Motivational

INSPIRATIONAL

ETHEA S. BROWN

PRIMIX
PUBLISHING
THE WRITE CHOICE

Primix Publishing
11620 Wilshire Blvd
Suite 900, West Wilshire Center, Los Angeles, CA, 90025
www.primixpublishing.com
Phone: 1-800-538-5788

Published by Primix Publishing: 05/31/2024

ISBN: 979-8-89194-137-3(sc)
ISBN: 979-8-89194-138-0(hc)
ISBN: 979-8-89194-139-7(e)

Library of Congress Control Number: 2024905158

To my family:

Willie Joe Brown

my mother Edan M.Sanders,

my Children, Lester, Eric, Yvonne,

Elder C. Jennings (U.H.O.P.F.A.P)

Prophet Shamar J. Bennett (Power
and Praise Ministries)

Deacon, Virgin Johnson SR. (Goodwill
Missionary Baptist Church)

my (8) Brothers. and (2) sisters.

Avery special Thank you, For being there and
helping me and encouraging me over the years.

When God Is In the Plan,
We don't see it, But God
Is working in our favor, to
God Glory, Honor, and
all Praises, Yes Lord, I am
Thankful to You Daily.

"The Lord shall command
the blessing upon the thee
in tiny storehouse, and in all
that thou settest thine hand
unto, and he shall bless thee
in the land witch the Lord
thy God giventh thee"

By: Ethel Brown Dandy

Psalms 91:1

"He that dwelleth in the secret place of the most. High shall abide under the shadow of the Almighty"

King James Version (KJV)

< > ▲ View Chapter

Psalms 91:1 Context

1He that dwelleth in the secret place of the most. High shall abide under the shadow of the Almighty. 2I will say of the LORD, He is my refuge and my fortress: my God; in him will I trust. 3Surely he shall deliver thee from the snare of the fowler, and the noisome pestilence. 4He shall cover thee with his feathers, and under his wings shalt thou trust: shall be thy shield and buckler.

Amen Amen Amen Thank you Jesus, yes God have your way In Jesus name. Walking in faith, not by sight, always keeping God First Daily. Cover me in your presence, protection, Father and strength, support me and surround me in your favor, grace, peace, mercy, love, patience, prayer, prophecy, prosperity, abundance, blessings, encouragement, wisdom, knowledge understanding, prosperity in prayer, fill with happiness, love, joy, peace, energy, humility, humbleness, grace and mercy, establishing my going out and coming In Jesus name, overcoming all negativity, over me. My children, grandchildren, grate grandchildren, seen and unseen, according to psalms 91, psalms 23, psalms 27, and psalms 64. Coverings is in your Anointed power, Favor, and multiply. Amen, thank you Jesus.

Psalms 64:1

"(To the chief Musician, A psalm of David.) Hear my voice, O God, in my prayer: preserve my life from fear of the enemy."

King James Version (KJV)

< > ▲ View Chapter

Psalms 64:1 Context

1(To the chief Musician of David.) Hear my voice, O God, in my prayer: preserve my life from fear of the enemy. 2Hide me from the secret counsel of the wicked; from the insurrection of the workers of iniquity: 3Who whet their tongue like a sword, and bend their bows to shoot their arrows, even bitter words: 4That they may shoot in secret at the perfect: suddenly do they shoot at him, and fear not. Amen 🙏 Thank you Jesus Lord Jesus I am thankful to you daily, I give you all Honor, and Praises. In Jesus name.

Daniel 2:19

"Then was the secret revealed unto Daniel in a night vision. Then Daniel blessed the God of heaven."

King James Version (KJV)

< > ▲ View Chapter

Daniel 2:19 Context

16Then Daniel went in, and desired of the king that he would give him time, and that he would shew the king the interpretation. 17Then Daniel went to his house, and made the thing known to Hananiah, Mishael, and Azariah, his companions: 18That they would desire mercies of God of heaven concerning this secret; that Daniel and his fellows should not perish with the rest of the wise men of Babylon. 19Then was the secret revealed unto Daniel in a night vision. The Daniel blessed the God of heaven. 20Daniel answered and said, Blessed be the name of God for ever and ever: for wisdom and might are his: 21And he changeth the times and the seasons: he removeth kings, and setteth up kings: he given wisdom unto the wise, and knowledge to them that know understanding: 22He revealeth the deep and secret things: he knoweth what is in the darkness, and the light dwelleth with him.

Proverbs 16:7

"When man's ways please the LORD, he maketh even his enemies to be at peace with him."

King James Version (KJV)

< > ▲ View Chapter

Proverbs 16:7 Context

4The LORD hath made all things for himself: yea, even the wicked for the day foe evil. 5Every one that is proud in heart is an abomination to the LORD: though hand join in hand, he shall not be unpunished. 6By mercy and truth iniquity is purged: and by the fear of the LORD men depart from evil. 7When a man's ways please the LORD, he maketh even his enemies to be at peace with him. 8Better is a little with righteous than great revenues without right. 9A man's heart deviseth his way: but the LORD directeth his steps. 10A divine sentences is in the lips of the king: his mouth transgresseth not in judgement.

Psalms 117:1

"O praise the LORD, all ye nations: praise him, all ye people."

King James Version (KJV)

< > ▲ View Chapter

Psalm 117:1 Context

10Praise the LORD, all ye nations: praise him, all ye people. 2For his merciful kindness is great toward us: and the truth of the LORD endureth for ever. Praise ye the LORD. Amen , Amen Thank you Jesus, yes Lord, Have your way.

Thank you Father for this amazing opportunity to share this beautiful new day, in Jesus name, thank you for giving your Angels charge to keep us safe from evil spirits, and danger, for delivering me from all evil minds of those that don't have my best interest, and intentions in their heart, mind, and soul. Thank you father for making away, for me, my children, grandchildren, grate grandchildren, true family members and friends, thank you for all the many blessings you have given us, from the smallest to the largest, thank you for strengthening us, guiding and leading, helping, protecting, understanding us and defending, delivering, and supporting, providing, and speaking to us, supporting and fighting our battles, for all our lives, thank you for faithfulness, wisdom, knowledge, kindness, compassion, faith, love, prayer, peace, gratitude, grace, and mercy, and prosperity, thank you Father for showing me how to take what you have given me, understanding and uplifting, using it wisely and giving you all Honor and Praise, and Glory, thank you for choosing and continuing to cover me in your prayers, and anointing positive light, and power in Jesus Name I have prayed. Amen , Amen, Amen. Thank you Jesus, Lord have your way. Work it out. Thank you for everything, establishing my gratitude going forward, as I am going in, and coming out, with all the right people for all the right reasons and righteousness purposes.

Psalms 23:1

"(A psalm of David.) The LORD is my shepherd; I shall not want."

King James Version (KJV)

< > ▲ View Chapter

Psalm 23:1 Context

1(A psalm of David.) The LORD is my shepherd; I shall not want. 2He maketh me to lie down in green pastures: he leadeth me beside the still waters. 3He retoreth my soul: he leadeth me in the paths of righteousness for his mane's sake. 4Yea, though I walk through the valley of the shadow of death, I will fear no evil: for thou art with me; thy rod and thy staff they comfort me.

Amen Amen Thank you Jesus yes.

Psalm 91:1

"He that dwelleth in the secret place of most High shall abide under shadow of the Almighty."

King James Version (KJV)

< > ▲ View Chapter

Psalm 91:1 Context

1He that dwelleth in the secret place of the most High shall abide under the shadow of the Almighty. 2I will say of the LORD, He is my refuge and my fortress: my God; in him will I trust. 3Surely he shall deliver thee from the snare of the fowler, and from noisome pestilence. 4He shall cover thee with his feathers, and under his wings shalt thou trust: his truth shall be shield and buckler.

Hebrews 12:25

"See that ye refuse not him that speaketh. For if they escaped not who refuse him that spake on earth, much more shall not we escape, if we turn away from him that speaketh from heaven."

King James Version (KJV)

< > ▲ View Chapter

Hebrews 12:25 Context

22But ye are come unto mout Sion, and unto the city of living God, the heavenly Jerusalem, and to an innumerable company of angels, 23To general assembly and church of the firstborn, which are written in heaven, and to God the Judge of all, and to the spirits of just men made perfect, 24And to Jesus the mediator of the covenant, and to the blood of sprinkling, that speaketh better things than that of Abel. 25See that ye refuse not him that speaketh. For if they escaped not who refuse him that spake on earth, much more shall not we escape, if we turn away from him that speaketh from heaven: 26Whose voice then shook the earth: but now he hath promised, saying, Yet once more I shake not the earth only, but also heaven. 27And this word, yet once more, signefieth the removing of those things that are shaken, as of things that are made, that those things which cannot be shaken may remain. 28Wherefore we receiving a Kingdom which cannot be moved, let us have grace, whereby we may serve God acceptably with reverence and godly fear:

Deuteronomy 6:15

For the LORD thy God is a jealous God among you)
lest the anger of the LORD thy God be kindled against,
and destroy thee from off the face of the earth."

King James Version (KJV)

< > ▲ View Chapter

Deuteronomy 6:15 Context

12Then beware lest thou forget the LORD, which
brought thee forth of the land of Egypt, from the house
of bondage. 13Thou shalt fear the LORD thy God, and
serve him, and shalt swear by his name. 12Ye shall not
go after other gods, of the gods of the people which are
round about you; 15(For the LORD thy God is a jealous
God among you) lest the anger of the LORD thy God
be kindled against thee, and destroy thee from off the
face of the earth. 16Ye shall not tempt the LORD your
God, as ye tempted him Massah. 17Ye shall diligently
keep the commandments of the LORD your God,
and his testimonies, and his statutes, which ha hath
commanded thee. 18And thou shalt do that which is
right and good in the right and good sight of the LORD:
that it may be well with thee, and that thou mayest go
in and possess the good land which the LORD sware
unto thy fathers,

Amen Thank you Jesus.

Titus 2:11

"For the grace of God that Brineth salvation hath appeared to all men"

King James Version (KJV)

< > ▲ View Chapter

Titus 2:11 Context

8Sound speech, that cannot be condemned; that he that is of the contrary part may be ashamed, having no evil thing to say of you. 9Exhort servants to be obedient unto their own masters, and to please them well in all things, not answering again; 10Not purloining, but shewing all good fidelity; that they may adorn the doctrine of God our Saviour in all things. 11For the grace of God that bringeth salvation hath appeared to all men, 12Teaching us that, denying ungoldliness and worldly lusts, we should live soberly, righteously, and godly, in this present world; 13Looking for that blessed hope, and the glorious appearing of the great God and our Savior Jesus Christ; 14Who gave himself for us, that he might redeem us from all inquiry, and purify unto himself a peculiar people, zealous of good works. Amen. Thank you Jesus. Yes God.

Thank you Lord for this opportunity to serve you in the beauty of Holiness today, Tomorrow, and going forward n Jesus name in the future in faith, love, peace, grace and mercy, wisdom, knowledge, understanding, compassion, courage, prayer, continue protecting, prosperous, prosperity, health, happiness, comfort, covered in the glory, prosperity, strength, safety, spiritual, strength in the Anointing positive spirit, of light, walking and living on God, Grace, abundance's officials, Devine teacher . And choose vesual

Continue to charge your Anointed powerful Angels to guider, lead, provide, support, protect, me, my children, grandchildren, grate grandchildren, true, faithful Family Members, and friends. In Jesus name, I have prayed.

Micah 7:7

"Therefore I will look unto the LORD; I will ait for the God of my salvations: my God will hear me."

King James Version (KJV)

< > ▲ View Chapter

Micah 7:7 Context

4The best of them is as brier: the most upright is sharper than a thorn hedge; the day of thy watchmen and thy visitation cometh; now shall be their perplexity. 5Trust ye not in a friend, put ye not confidence in a guide: keep the doors of thy mouth from her that lieth in thy bosom. 6For against the son dishonoreth the father, the daughter riseth up against her mother, the daughter in law against her mother in law; a man's enemies are he men of his own house. 7Therefore I will unto the LORD; I will wait for the God of my salvation: my God will hear me. 8Rejoice not against me, O mine enemy: when I fall, I shall arise; when I sit in darkness, the LORD shall be a light unto me. 9I will bear the indigination of the LORD, because I have sinned against him, until he plead my cause, execute judgement for me: he will bring forth the light, and I shall behold his righteousness. 10Then she that is mine enemy shall see it, and shame shall cover her which said unto me, Where is the LORD thy God? Mine eyes shall behold her: now shall she be trodden down as the mire of the streets.

Amen Amen Amen Thank you Jesus.

"The thief cometh not, but for to steal, and to kill, and to destroy: I am come that they might have life, and that they might have it more abundantly." John 10:10 KJV

Psalm 27:1

"(A Psalm od David.) The LORD is my light and my salvation; whom shall I fear? LORD is the strength of my life; of whom shall I be afraid?"

King James Version (KJV)

< > ▲ View Chapter

Psalm 27:1 Context

(A Psalm od David.) The LORD is my light and my salvation; whom shall I fear? LORD is the strength of my life; of whom shall I be afraid? 2When the wicked, even mine enemies and my foes, came upon me to eat up my fleash, they stumbled and fell. 3Though an host should encamp against me, my heart shall not fear: though war should ride against me, in this will I be confident. 4One thing have I desired of the LORD, that will seek after; that I may dwell in the house of the LORD all the days of my life, to behold the beauty of the LORD, to enquire in his temple. Amen Amen Thank you Jesus, yes LORD.

Thank you Father for this beautiful gift of grace love, peace, grace and mercy, healing, health, and a sound mind, strength, wisdom, knowledge, understanding, kindness, compassion, comfort, patience, prosperity, protection, provision, courage, and unwavering faith, and the must endure and pass through one day.

Hold on family, be strong and pray we are not alone, God is with us, we are not going through alone.

Everyday, with God, in our life is sweeter than the day before, Walking in the faith, not by sight, always keeping God first daily.

Psalm23, 27, 91 and the prayer and wisdom, knowledge, understanding, unity, in prosperous, prosperity, in the Anointing Spirit of God covering, God guiding Principles, which light, our eyes, mind, heart, soul. In Jesus name I have prayed. Amen

Walking in the faith
Not by sight, always keeping
God fist daily. Thankful.

Good morning everyone

Welcome to 2024. Happy new year!

Thank you Father for allowing us to cross over into 2014, thank your for watching over us in 2023, and for all of your blessings, guidance, leadership, teaching, support, providing, supporting, helping us all to make better decisions, and becoming better people, thank you for giving us your angels charge to keep me safe from all harm and sickness, evil, and death and destruction, thank you for sending all the right people, right righteous people, for all the right reason, and purpose, thank you for opening up all doors that may have been closed by evil, people that did not have our best interest, and intentions, in their hearts mind and spirit and souls, thank you for offering doors that no one else but you can close. Thank you for all the wisdom, knowledge, understanding, you have entrusted me with and for showing me how to use them wisely, thank you for my children, grandchildren, grate grandchildren.

And all my family members and friends, thank you for everything, and establishing me going forward, in your words covering with love, grace, mercy, kindness, compassion, respect for others and for myself. Thank you for blessing the little I had and showing me how to use it wisely, and making it to multiply, healing, my heart, body, mind and soul, strengthening me, encouraging me, not to give up over the years, thank you for blessing me and keeping me in your presence, in your will and in your way. In Jesus name I have prayed, yes, God have your way, Amen.

Walking in faith, not by sight. Always keeping God first Daily.

No weapon formed against us shall prosper, accepting to God words, thank you Jesus for your amazing teaching and covering in you anointing power and Amazing Grace, providing, protecting, supporting, guiding and leading in wisdom, teaching, yes LORD.

Deuteronomy 6:2

"That thou mightiest fear the LORD thy Gd, to keep all his statutes and his commandments, which I command thee, thou, and thy son, and thy son's son, all the days of thy life; and that thy days maybe prolonged."

King James Version (KJV)

< > ▲ View Chapter

Deuteronomy 6:2 Context

1Now these are the commandments, the statutes, and the judgements, which the LORD your God commanded to teach you, that ye might do them in the land whither ye go posses it: 2That thou mightiest far the LORD thy God, to keep all his statutes and his commandments, which I command thee, thou, and thy son, and thy son's son, all the days of thy life; and that thy days maybe prolonged. 3Hear therefore. O Israel, and observe to do it; that it maybe well thee, and that ye may increase mightily as the LORD God of thy fathers hath promised thee, in the land that floweth with milk and honey. 4Hear, O Israel: The LORD our God is one LORD:5And thou shalt love the LORD thy God with all thine heart, and with all thy soul, and with all thy might. Amen Amen Amen. Thank you Jesus yes. LORD

Good morning everyone,

Thank you dear God for this new day, as I got forward in this new day, give you Angels charge to keep me salty in you care, away from all forms of evil and danger seen and unseen, keep me, my children, grandchildren. Grate grandchildren true family members and friends, cover us all in your loving care and support, peace, grace and mercy and Anointing power in protecting our every footsteps, and establishing out pathways in your way and your will. In Jesus name I have prayed. Amen Amen Amen Thank you Jesus, yes LORD.

Psalm 37:1

"(A psalm of David.) Fret not thyself because of evildoers, neither be thou envious against the workers of iniquity."

King James Version (KJV)

< > ▲ View Chapter

Deuteronomy 6:2 Context

1(A psalm of David.) Fret not thyself because of evildoers, neither be thou envious against the workers of iniquity. 2For they shall soon be cut downlike the grass, and wither as green herb. 3Trust in the LORD, and do good; so shalt thou dwell in the land, and verily thou shalt be fed. 4Delight thyself also in the LORD; and he shall give thee the desires of thine heart.

2 Thessalonians 3:2

"And that we may be delivered from unreasonable and wicked men: for all men have not faith."

King James Version (KJV)

< > ▲ View Chapter

2 Thessalonians 3:2 Context

1Finally, brethren, pray for us, that the word of the LORD may have free course, and be glorified, even as it is with you:2And that we may be delivered from unreasonable and wicked men: for all men have not faith. 3But the LORD is faithful, who shall stablish you, and keep you from evil. 4And we have confidence in the Lord touching you, that ye both do and will do the things which we command you. 5And the Lord direct your hearts into the love of God, and into the patient waiting for Christ.

Amen Amen Amen Thank you Jesus. Yes Lord.

Good morning everyone,

Thank you dear God, for blessing us to witness this beautiful day, thank you for all of your prayer and blessings, as we move forward in celebrating this beautiful blessed day with our family and friends, send your Angels to encamp all around us all and fill our hearts with love, peace, joy, happiness, relief, kindness, compassion, comfort, respect, forgiveness, thankfulness and faith in our country, and our nation, future, provision, prosperity, freedom, favor, and justice for all of your children, keep me safe from all situations that is not of you and from you, seen and unseen. Continue to protect, and send all the right people into our hearts, country, nation, community, and world for all eternity, for all the right reasons and right purposes. Thank you Father for covering me in your prayers and wisdom and wings of Anointing positive power and strength, guidance with your light, divine mercy and grace. In Jesus name I have prayed.

Amen Amen Amen Amen Thank you Jesus. Yes God, have your way.

Daniel 4:26

"And whereas they commended to leave the stump of the tree roots; thy kingdom sha; be sure unto thee, after that thou shalt have known that heavens do rule."

King James Version (KJV)

< > ▲ View Chapter

Daniel 4:26 Context

23And whereas the king saw a watcher and a holy one coming down from heaven, and saying, Hew the tree down, and destroy it; yet leave the stump of the roots thereof in the earth, even with a band of iron and brass, in the tender grass of the field; and let it be wet with dew of heaven, and let his portion be with the beast of the field, till seven times pass over him; 24This is the interpretation, O king, and this is the decree of the most High, which is come upon my lord the king: 25That they shall drive thee from men, and thy dwelling shall be with beasts of the field, and they shall make thee to eat grass as oxen, and they shall wet thee with the dew of heaven, and even times shall pass over thee, till thou know that the most High ruleth in the kingdom of men, and giveth it to whomsoever he will. 26And whereas they commanded to leave the stump of the tree roots; thy kingdom shall be sure unto thee, and break off thy sins by righteousness, and thine iniquities by shewing mercy to the por; if it may be a lengthening of thy tranquillity.

28All this came upon the king Nebuchadnezzar. 29At the end of twelve months he walked of the kingdom of Babylon. Amen

Thank you Jesus. Yes God

ebd

Psalms 23:1

"(A Psalm of David.) The LORD is my shepherd; I shall not want."

King James Version (KJV)

ebd

Deuteronomy 8:19

"And it shall be, if thou do at all forget the LORD thy God, and walk after other gods, and serve them, and worship them, I testify against you this day that ye shall surely perish."

King James Version (KJV)

< > ▲ View Chapter

Deuteronomy 8:19 Context

16Who fed thee in the wilderness with manna, which thy fathers knew not, that he might humble thee, and that he might prove thee, to do thee good at thy latter end; 17And thou say in thine heart, My power and the might of mine hand hath gotten me this wealth. 18But thou shalt remember the LORD thy God: for it is he that giveth thee power to get wealth, that he may establish his covenant which he sware unto thy fathers, as it is this day. 19And it shall be, if thou do at all forget the LORD thy God, and walk after other gods, and serve them, and worship them, I testify against you this day that ye shall surely perish. 20As the nations which the LORD destroyeth before your face, so shall ye perish; because ye would not be obedient unto the voice of the LORD your God. Amen Thank you Jesus, yes LORD,

I am praying Amen and thank you Jesus Christ for your prayers, service, support, guidance, encouragement, protection, compassion, love, gratitude Grace, Mercy, peace, wisdom, patience, prosperity, provision, caring, healing, determination, deliverance. From all evil, deeds of the enemies, thank you for choosing me covering me in your arms, under your wings, in Anointing positive power of protection, and establishing my character, courage, compassion, trust, commitment, loyalty, in your will and your way, as I am told, coming in and going out. Again I thank you for all the wisdom, knowledge, and understanding you have provided, and entrusted me with to use wisely, thanks you for providing and protecting me, my children, e in haven grandchildren, grate grandchildren, true family members and friends. In Jesus name I pray Amen Amen thank you Jesus.

Our Father Which are in heaven and earth, you will be done, and forgive us, as we forever

those who trust pass against us, lead us not into temptation, but deliver us from darkness and evil, with your guidance walking in the light understanding your Father.

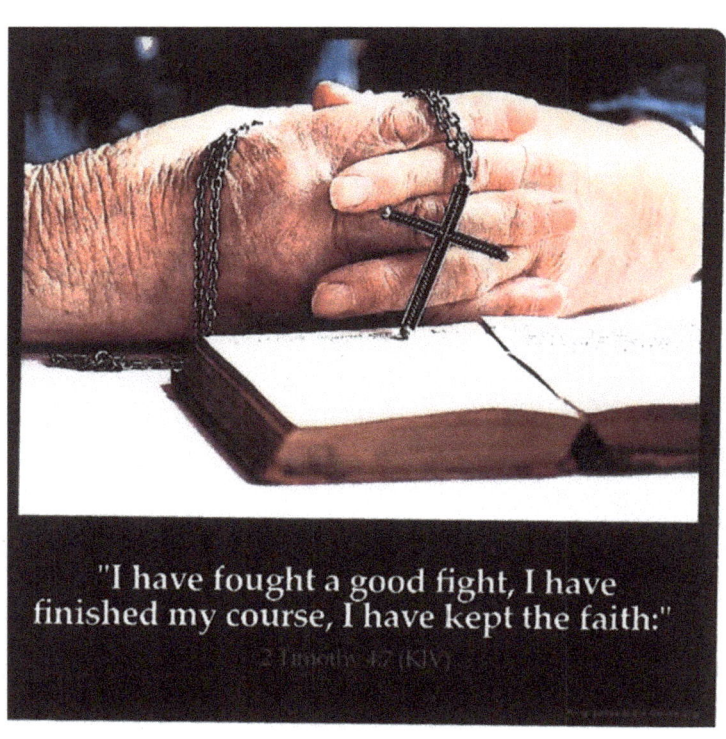

"I have fought a good fight, I have finished my course, I have kept the faith:"

2 Timothy 4:7 (KJV)

Daniel 2:19

"Then was the secret revealed unto Daniel in a night vision. Then Daniel blessed the God of heaven."

King James Version (KJV)

< > ▲ View Chapter

Daniel 2:19 Context

16Then Daniel went in, and desired of the king that he would give him time, and that he would shew the king the interpretation. 17Then Daniel went to his house, and made the thing known to Hananiah, Mishael, and Azariah, his companions: 18That they would desire mercies of the God of heaven concerning this secret; that Daniel and his fellows should not perish with the rest of the wise men of Babylon. 19Then was the secret revealed unto Daniel in a night vision. Then Daniel blessed the God of heaven. 20Daniel answered and said, Blessed be the name of God for ever and ever: for wisdom and might are his: 21And he changeth the times and the seasons: he removeth kings, and setteth up kings: he giveth wisdom unto the wise, and knowledge to them that know understanding: 22He revealeth the deep and secret things: he knoweth what is in the darkness, and the light dwelleth with him.

Good morning everyone,

Thank you God You watch over me all night and wake me up in my right mind, health, and spirit, soul and strength, as I go forward in this day, Father walking in faith, give your Angels charge to guide, lead, protect me, my children, grandchildren, grate grandchildren, true family members, and friends, from all evil, and danger, seen and unseen, opening all the right doors and gates, that only you have the power to open, and closing all doors and gates that are not from you and of you, keeping all those that don't have my best interests, and intentions in their hearts, mind, soul and wishes to do me, my children, grandchildren, grate grandchildren, harm continue to cover me in your heart, prayers, and Anointing power, and protection, in your grace, mercy, wisdom, knowledge, understanding, open my eyes, ears, to see what you would have me to see and hear what you would have me to hear, establish my gratitude and thanks daily, going in , and coming out, with all the right people for all the right reasons, and purpose, thank you Father, for grace and mercy, the Holy Ghost, spiritual guidance and healing, deliverance, from all those that don't have my best interest in mind, and heart. In Jesus name I have prayed, Amen Amen.

Amen Thank you Jesus, Yes Lord.

ebd

Thank you Father for this new day, allowing me to give you thanks and Praises, all Honor and Glory belongs to you, as we go forward continue to cover me in Abundance, health, happiness, joy, peace, love, prayers prosperity, provision, and your Anointing Grace and mercy.in Jesus I pray.

Thank you, father for this day as we go forward, send your angels protection to guide lead and protect me from all sin, and on scene, evil and danger, and all those that don't have my best interest in their hearts, mind, body and soul cover me under your wings of protection in your anointed power of grace, love, peace, prosperity, deliverance, business, knowledge, and understanding guide my airship in Jesus name I pray. Amen. ebd

Job 9:12

"Behold, he taketh away, who can hinder him? who will say unto him, What doesn't thou?"

King James Version (KJV)

< > ▲ View Chapter

Job 9:12 Context

9Which maketh Arcturus, Orion, and Pleiades, and the chambers of the south. 10Which doeth great things past finding out; yea, and wonders without number. 11Lo, he goeth by me, and I see him not: he passeth on also, but I perceive him not. 12Behold, he taketh away, who can hinder him? who will say unto him, What doesn't thou? 13If God will not withdraw his anger, the proud helpers do stoop under him. 14How much less shall I answer him, and choose out my words to reason with him? 1SWhom, though I were righteous, yet would I not answer, but I would make supplication to my judge. Amen thank you Jesus. ebd

Matthew 6:33

"But seek ye first the kingdom of God, and his righteousness; and all these things shall be added unto you."

King James Version (KJV)

< > ▲ View Chapter

Matthew 6:33 Context

30Wherefore, if God so clothe the grass of the field, which to day is, and to morrow is cast into the oven, shall he not much more clothe you, 0 ye of little faith? 31Therefore take no thought, saying, What shall we eat? or, What shall we drink? or, Wherewithal shall we be clothed? 32(For after all these things do the Gentiles seek:) for your heavenly Father knoweth that ye have need of all these things. 33But seek ye first the kingdom of God, and his righteousness; and all these things shall be added unto you. 34Take therefore no thought for the morrow: for the morrow shall take thought for the things of itself. Sufficient unto the day is the evil thereof. Amen thank you Jesus yes God

ebd

"The thief cometh not, but for to steal, and to kill, and to destroy: I am come that they might have life, and that they might have it more abundantly." John 10:10 KJV

ebd

Matthew 6:33

"But seek ye first the kingdom of God, and his righteousness; and all these things shall be added unto you."

King James Version (KJV)

< > ▲ View Chapter

Matthew 6:33 Context

30Wherefore, if God so clothe the grass of the field, which today is, and tomorrow is cast into the oven, shall he not much more clothe you, O ye of little faith? 31Therefore take no thought, saying, What shall we eat? or, What shall we drink? or, Wherewithal shall we be clothed? 32(For after all these things do the Gentiles seek:) for your heavenly Father knoweth that ye have need of all these things. 33But seek ye first the kingdom of God, and his righteousness; and all these things shall be added unto you. 34Take therefore no thought for the morrow: for the morrow shall take thought for the things of itself. Sufficient unto the day is the evil thereof.

Amen thank you Jesus yes God

ebd

Dear God,
I did not sleep well,
but I did wake up.
My wallet isn't full,
but my belly is.
I may not have all I want,
but I have all I need.
My life isn't perfect,
but my life is good.
Thank You!
~Amen~

Everyday with God in my life is sweeter than the day before. Yes God, Thank you God.

Enjoy a safe and blessed
Father's Day, everyone.

Thank you dear God, for this new blessed day, thank you for watching over me all night long and for waking me up in my right mind, health, and spirit, soul and Strength. As I go forward into this day journey, send your Angels, before, beside, behind, beneath, above, and all around me, my children, grandchildren, and grate grandchildren, family members and friends, protecting us from all forms of evil, and all dangers situations, that tries to come our way that is not of you.

Give your Angels charge to guide us through all temptation, deliver us from all evil, and those that don't have our best intentions in their hearts and minds. In Jesus name I have prayed Amen, thank you Jesus, yes God I am thankful, to you, for all of your many blessings, seen and unseen, from the last to the greatest continue to order my footsteps in your will and your way, giving your Anointing power, of Grace, mercy, protection, peace, love and abundance, all the right people for all the right reasons and for all the right purposes into my life, I give you all humor, and all Praises. Amen send you Anointing, positive power, kindness and keeping my faith, heart, mind in your spirit always, yes, Lord, thank you Jesus.

Thank you dear God for this new day, a day i have not seen before, as I go forward in this new day and new week, give your Angels charge to Guide and Lead my footsteps, protecting my family, my children,, grandchildren, grate grandchildren, myself and others, keep us all safe in your care, and under your wings, of protection, from all seen and unseen, danger, and suffering, and evil, and from all those that don't have our best interest in their hearts and minds, in Jesus name I have prayed, God, to your will, and to your will. Not my will, but you will be done on earth as it is in heaven. Forgive us, as we forgive all those who have trust passed against us, and deliver, us from all evil and give us our daily bread; and, us, fill me with your strength, love, Grace, peace, mercy, in your Holy Ghost Anointed power, and protection from all evil, seen and unseen. Yest God, Amen thank you. No weapons from against us shall never prosper, nor shall ever come to pass.

Corinthians 3:13

"Every man's work shall be made manifest: for the day shall declare it, because it shall be revealed by fire; and the fire shall try every man's work of what sort it is."

King James Version (KJV)

< > ▲ View Chapter

1 Corinthians 3:13 Context

10According to the grace of God which is given unto me, as a wise masterbuilder, I have laid the foundation, and another buildeth thereon. But let every man take heed how he buildeth thereupon. 11For other foundation can no man lay than that is laid, which is Jesus Christ. 12Now if any man build upon this foundation gold, silver, precious stones, wood, hay, stubble; 13Every man's work shall be made manifest: for the day shall declare it, because it shall be revealed by fire; and the fire shall try every man's work of what sort it is. 14If any man's work abide which he hath built thereupon, he shall receive a reward. 15If any man's work shall be burned, he shall suffer loss: but he himself shall be saved; yet so as by fire. I 6Know ye not that ye arc the temple of God, and that the Spirit of God dwelleth in you Amen thank you Jesus

ebd

2 Chronicles 13:5

"Ought ye not to know that the LORD God of Israel gave the kingdom over Israel to David for ever, even to him and to his sons by a covenant of salt?"

King James Version (KJV)

< > ▲ View Chapter

2 Chronicles 13:5 Context

2He reigned three years in Jerusalem. His mother's name also was Michaiah the daughter of Uriel of Gibeah. And there was war between Abijah and Jeroboam. 3And Abijah set the battle in array with an army of valiant men of war, even four hundred thousand chosen men: Jeroboam also set the battle in array against him with eight hundred thousand chosen men, being mighty men of valour. 4And Abijah stood up upon mount Zemaraim, which is in mount Ephraim, and said, Hear me, thou Jeroboam, and all Israel; sought ye not to know that the LORD God of Israel gave the kingdom over Israel to David forever, even to him and to his sons by a covenant of salt? 6Yet Jeroboam the son of Nebat, the servant of Solomon the son of David, is risen up, and hath rebelled against his lord. 7And there are gathered unto him vain men, the children of Belia!, and have strengthened themselves against Rehoboam the son of Solomon, when Rehoboam was young and tenderhearted, and could not withstand them. 8And now ye think to withstand the kingdom of the LORD in the hand of the sons of David; and ye be a great multitude, and there are with you golden calves, which Jeroboam made you for gods. Amen, thank you. Jesus, I am grateful to you daily ebd

Genesis 41:12

"And there was there with us a young man, an Hebrew, servant to the captain of the guard; and we told him, and he interpreted to us our dreams: to each man according to his dream he did interpret."

King James Version (KN)

< > ▲ View Chapter

Genesis 41:12 Context

9Then spake the chief butler unto Pharaoh, saying, I do remember my faults this day: 10Pharaoh was wroth with his servants, and put me in ward in the captain of the guard's house, both me and the chief baker: 11And we dreamed a dream in one night, I and he; we dreamed each man according to the interpretation of his dream. 12And there was there with us a young man, an Hebrew, servant to the captain of the guard; and we told him, and he interpreted to us our dreams; to each man according to his dream he did interpret. 13And it came to pass, as he interpreted to us, so it was; me he restored unto mine office, and him he hanged. 14Then Pharaoh sent and called Joseph, and they brought him hastily out of the dungeon: and he shaved himself, and changed his raiment, and came in unto Pharaoh. I 5And Pharaoh said unto Joseph, I have dreamed a dream, and there is none that can interpret it: and I have heard say of thee, that thou canst understand a dream to interpret it.

Thank you father for this new day, as I go froward Father please give your angels charge to watch over me my children, grandchild, great grandchildren , friends, and family, order our footsteps in your will and way, keeping us safe from all those who don't have our best intentions and interest at their hearts and minds; thank you Father for covering me in your anointing power, grace and mercy, in Jesus name I pray.ebd

Peter 1:11

"Searching what, or what manner of time the Spirit of Christ which was in them did signify, when it testified beforehand the sufferings of Christ, and the glory that should follow."

King James Version (KN)

< > ▲ View Chapter

1 Peter 1:11 Context

8Whom having not seen, ye love; in whom, though now ye see him not, yet believing, ye rejoice with joy unspeakable and full of glory: 9Receiving the end of your faith, even the salvation of your souls. 10Of which salvation the prophets have enquired and searched diligently, who prophesied of the grace that should come unto you: 11Searching what, or what manner of time the Spirit of Christ which was in them did signify, when it testified beforehand the sufferings of Christ, and the glory that should follow. 12Unto whom it was revealed, that not unto themselves, but unto us they did minister the things, which are now reported unto you by them that have preached the gospel unto you with the Holy Ghost sent down from heaven; which things the angels desire to look into.

13Wherefore gird up the loins of your mind, be sober, and hope to the end for the grace that is to be brought unto you at the revelation of Jesus Christ; 14As obedient children, not fashioning yourselves according to the former lusts in your ignorance:

Amen thank you Jesus for your prayers today and for your support and love going forward, continue covering me, my children, grandchildren, grate grandchildren, true family members and friends, keeping us safe from all those that don't have our best interest in their hearts and minds. Thank you Father for continuing to cover me in your Amazing Anointed Grace and Mercy. In Jesus name I have prayed, yes, Father I thank you

ebd

Deuteronomy 28:1

"And it shall come to pass, if thou shalt hearken diligently unto the voice of the LORD thy God, to observe and to do all his commandments which I command thee this day, that the LORD thy God will set thee on high above all nations of the earth:"

King James Version (KJV)

< > ▲ View Chapter

Deuteronomy 28:1 Context

1And it shall come to pass, if thou shalt hearken diligently unto the voice of the LORD thy God, to observe and to do all his commandments which I command thee this day, that the LORD thy God will set thee on high above all nations of the earth: 2And all these blessings shall come on thee, and overtake thee, if thou shalt hearken unto the voice of the LORD thy God. 3Blessed shalt thou be in the city, and blessed shalt thou be in

the field. 4Blessed shall be the fruit of thy body, and the fruit of thy ground, and the fruit of thy cattle, the increase of thy kine, and the flocks of thy sheep. Amen thank you Jesus.

ebd

Isaiah 54:17

"No weapon that is formed against thee shall prosper; and every tongue that shall rise against thee in judgment thou shalt condemn. This is the heritage of the servants of the LORD, and their righteousness is of me, saith the LORD."

King James Version (KJV) ebd

"We are not Indians we are Native Americans, we are older than both concepts. We are people, We are human Beings."

Ansvarr Wilhelm Ahlstrom

They couldn't be any more human than their ancestors whom crossed the Bering Strait from Eurasia to the Americas to bring them up onto the land of "freedom".

Jenny Wehrle Cleckner

Cherokee Women and Their Important Roles:

Women in the Cherokee society were equal to men. They could earn the title of War Women and sit in councils as equals. This privilege led an Irishman named Adair who traded with the Cherokee from 1736-1743 to accuse the Cherokee of having a "petticoat government".

Clan kinship followed the mother's side of the family. The children grew up in the mother's house, and it was the duty of an uncle on the mother's side to teach the boys how to hunt, fish, and perform certain tribal duties. The women owned the houses and their furnishings. Marriages were carefully negotiated, but if a woman decided to divorce her spouse, she simply placed his belongings outside the house. Cherokee women also worked hard. They cared for the children, cooked, tended the house, tanned skins, wove baskets, and cultivated the fields. Men helped with some household chores like sewing, but they spent most of their time hunting.

Cherokee girls learned by example how to be warriors and healers. They learned to weave baskets, tell stories, trade, and dance. They became mothers and wives, and learned their heritage. The Cherokee learned to adapt, and the women were the core of the Cherokee.

A True Leader Unites
People Not divide them. Do
not find faults, But finds
remedies. Do not show
hates, but cutivates love.

Thank you Father for this new day, bless us according to your words, wisdom, grace and mercy continue to shine on me, covering me in your presence Anointing positive power in you wings of wisdom, peace, prosperity, protection in Jesus name Amen end.

I started running. I started
praising God I have no reason
to doubt you God.
Ebd

"It is easier to build **strong children** than to repair broken men."

- Frederick Douglass

Romans 8:3

"For what the law could not do, in that it was weak through the flesh, God sending his own Son in the likeness of sinful flesh, and for sin, condemned sin in the flesh:"

King James Version (KJV)

< > ▲ View Chapter

Romans 8:3 Context

1There is therefore now no condemnation to them which are in Christ Jesus, who walk not after the flesh, but after the Spirit. 2For the law of the Spirit of life in Christ Jesus hath made me free from the law of sin and death. 3For what the law could not do, in that it was weak through the flesh, God sending his own Son in the likeness of sinful flesh, and for sin, condemned sin in the flesh: 4That the righteousness of the law might be fulfilled in us, who walk not after the flesh, but after the Spirit. 5For they that are after the flesh do mind the things of the flesh; but they that are after the Spirit the things of the Spirit. 6For to be carnally minded is death; but to be spiritually minded is life and peace. Amen thank you Jesus yes God.ebd.

Thank you Havenly Father for watching over me and my children , grandchildren, grate grandchildren, true family members and friends, for keeping us safe from evil spirits and dangers situations, from all those around us that don't have our best interest, and intentions in their hearts and minds, thank you Father for continuing to cover us in your prayers and Anointing of protection, prayers, prosperity, peace, provision, love, happiness healing a sound mind and your grace and mercy,, in Jesus name I pray Amen Amen Amen Yes protect us from all evil and danger seen and unseen. Ebd.

John 10:10

"The thief cometh not, but for to steal, and to kill, and to destroy: I am come that they might have life, and that they might have it more abundantly."

King James Version (KJV)

< > ▲ View Chapter

John 10:10 Context

7Then said Jesus unto them again, Verily, verily, I say unto you, I am the door of the sheep. 8Allthat ever came before me are thieves and robbers: but the sheep did not hear them. 91 am the door: by me if any man enter in, he shall be saved, and shall go in and out, and find pasture. 10The thief cometh not, but for to steal, and to kill, and to destroy: I am come that they might have life, and that they might have it more abundantly. 11I am the good shepherd: the good shepherd giveth his life for the sheep. 12But he that is an hireling, and not the shepherd, whose own the sheep are not, seeth the wolf coming, and leaveth the sheep, and fleeth: and the wolf catcheth them, and scattereth the sheep. 13The hireling fleeth, because he is an hireling, and careth not for the sheep. Amen Amen Amen and Amen thank you Jesus, yes God, I give you all my heart mind body and soul, continue to give your Angels charge to keep me alive and safe from all evil and danger seen and unseen, covered me. My children, grandchildren and grate grandchildren in your power and strength with your Anointing And Holy Ghost spirit, establish my life completely in all aspects.in your wisdom. Will and ways. In Jesus name I pray Amen ebd

ebd daily prayers.

Daniel 1:19

"And the king communed with them; and among them all was found none like Daniel, Hananiah, Mishael, and Azariah: therefore stood they before the king."

King James Version (KJV)

< > ▲ View Chapter

Daniel 1 :19 Context

16Thus Melzar took away the portion of their meat, and the wine that they should drink; and gave them pulse. 17 As for these four children, God gave them knowledge and skill in all learning and wisdom: and Daniel had understanding in all visions and dreams. 18Now at the end of the days that the king had said he should bring them in, then the prince of the eunuchs brought them in before Nebuchadnezzar. 19And the king communed with them; and among them all was found none like Daniel, Hananiah, Mishael, and Azariah: therefore stood they before the king. 20And in all matters of wisdom and understanding, that the king enquired of them, he found them ten times better than all the magicians and astrologers that were in all his realm. 21And Daniel continued even unto the first year of king Cyrus.

Amen thank you Jesus yes God.

Ebd

Mark 16:2

"And very early in the morning the first day of the week, they came unto the sepulchre at the rising of the sun."

King James Version (KJV)

2 Corinthians 5:1

"For we know that if our earthly house of this tabernacle were dissolved, we have a building of God, an house not made with hands, eternal in the heavens."

King James Version (KJV)

ebd

Psalm 16:1
"(Michtam of David.)
Preserve me, O God for in
thee do I put my trust."
King James Version (KJV)

Philippians 4:19

"But my God shall supply all your need according to his riches in glory by Christ Jesus."

King James Version (KJV)

< > ▲ View Chapter

Philippians 4:19 Context

16For even in Thessalonica ye sent once and again unto my necessity. 17Not because I desire a gift: but I desire fruit that may abound to your account. 18But I have all, and abound: I am full, having received of Epaphroditus the things which were sent from you, an odour of a sweet smell, a sacrifice acceptable, well pleasing to God. 19But my God shall supply all your need according to his riches in glory by Christ Jesus. 20Now unto God and our Father be glory for ever and ever. Amen. 21 Salute every saint in Christ Jesus. The brethren which are with me greet you. 22All the saints salute you, chiefly they that are of Caesar's household.

Thank you Father for another day and another great week ahead going forward in Jesus name, please continue to give your Angels charge to keep me safe from all situations, seen and unseen that is not of you, thank you for choosing and covering me, my children, grandchildren, grate grandchildren in your wings of protection, and establishing our relationship, and organizing our lives in your way and your will, in Jesus name I pray Amen Amen Amen and Amen yes, a God am thankful you daily

ebd

"We love and will receive them with open arms but to stay they going to have to be delivered. Don't bring back the same confusion you left with."

I copied and post this statement ebd

1 Thessalonians 5:18

"In every thing give thanks: for this is the will of God in Christ Jesus concerning you."

King James Version (KJV)

< > ▲ View Chapter

1 Thessalonians 5:18 Context

15See that none render evil for evil unto any man; but ever follow that which is good, both among yourselves, and to all men. 16Rejoice evermore. 17Pray without ceasing. 18In everything give thanks: for this is the will of God in Christ Jesus concerning you. 19Quench not the Spirit. 20Despise not prophesyings. 21 Prove all things; hold fast that which is good.

Amen thank you God.

1 Peter 1:16

"Because it is written, Be ye holy; for I am holy."

King James Version (KJV)

< > ▲ View Chapter

1 Peter 1 :16 Context

13Wherefore gird up the loins of your mind, be sober, and hope to the end for the grace that is to be brought unto you at the revelation of Jesus Christ; 14As obedient children, not fashioning yourselves according to the former lusts in your ignorance: 15But as he which hath called you is holy, so be ye holy in all manner of conversation; 16Because it is written, Be ye holy; for I am holy. 17And if ye call on the Father, who without respect of persons judgeth according to every man's work, pass the time of your sojourning here in fear: 18For as much as ye know that ye were not redeemed with corruptible things, as silver and gold, from your vain conversation received by tradition from your fathers; 19But with the precious blood of Christ, as of a lamb without blemish and without spot:

Amen.

"And it shall come to pass, if thou shalt hearken diligently unto the voice of the LORD thy God, to observe and to do all his commandments which I command thee this day, that the LORD thy God will set thee on high above all nations of the earth:" Deuteronomy 28:1 KJV

Psalms 65:6
"Which by his strength satteth
fast the mountains being
girded with power."
King James Version (KJV)

Never Believe everything someone tells you about a person without actually speaking with the person yourself and gathering all the facts. Ebd

Job 9:12

"Behold he taketh away, who can hinder him? Who will say unto him, What does thou?"

King James Version (KJV)

< > ▲ View Chapter

Job 9:12 Context

9Which maketh Arcturus, Orion, and Pleiades, and the chambers of the south. 10Which doeth great things fast finding out; yea, and wonders without number. 11Lo, he goeth by me, and I see him not: he passeth on also, but I perceive him not. 12Behold, he taketh away who can hinder him? Who will say unto hi, what does thou? 13If God will not withdraw his anger, the proud helpers do stoop under him. 14.How much less shall I answer him, and choose out my words to reason with him. 14How much less shall I answer him, and choose out my words to reason with him? 15Whom, though I were righteous, yet would I not answer, but I would make supplication to my judge.

Amen thank you Jesus. ebd

When your parents are not rich but still afford to give you a beautiful life.

Appreciate their sacrifices.

Thank you, father for this day as we go forward, send your angels protection to guide lead and protect me from all sin, and on scene, evil and danger, and all those that don't have my best interest in their hearts, mind, body and soul cover me under your wings of protection in your anointed power of grace, love, peace, prosperity, deliverance, business, knowledge, and understanding guide my airship in Jesus name I pray. Amen. Ebd

No matter how big your house is, how recent your car is, or how big your bank account is, our graves will all be the same size. Stay humble.

AMERICAN STORY

Everyday with God in my life is sweeter than the day before. thank you Jesus, Walking in faith, not by site, always keeping God first daily.ebd

"The thief cometh not, but for to steal, and to kill, and to destroy: I am come that they might have life, and that they might have it more abundantly." John 10:10 KJV

ebd

*

Matthew 6:33

"But seek ye first the kingdom of God, and his righteousness; and all these things shall be added unto you."

King James Version (KJV)

< > ▲ View Chapter

Matthew 6:33 Context

30Wherefore, if God so clothe the grass of the field, which to day is, and tomorrow is cast into the oven, shall he not much more clothe you, 0 ye of little faith? 31Therefore take no thought, saying, What shall we eat? or, What shall we drink? or, Wherewithal shall we be clothed? 32(For after all these things do the Gentiles seek:) for your heavenly Father knoweth that ye have need of all these things. 33But seek ye first the kingdom of God, and his righteousness; and all these things shall be added unto you. 34Take therefore no thought for the morrow: for the morrow shall take thought for the things of itself. Sufficient unto the day is the evil thereof. Amen thank you Jesus yes God.

•

Psalms 27:2

"When the wicked, even mine enemies and my foes, came upon me to eat up my flesh, they stumbled and fell."

King James Version (KJV

< > ▲ View Chapter

Psalms 27:2 Context

1 (A Psalm of David.) The LORD is my light and my salvation; whom shall I fear? the LORD is the strength of my life; of whom shall I be afraid? 2When the wicked, even mine enemies and my foes, came upon me to eat up my flesh, they stumbled and fell. 3Though an host should encamp against me, my heart shall not fear: though war should rise against me, in this will I be confident. 4One thing have I desired of the LORD, that will I seek after; that I may dwell in the house of the LORD all the days of my life, to behold the beauty of the LORD, and to enquire in his temple. 5For in the time of trouble he shall hide me in his pavilion: in the secret of his tabernacle shall he hide me; he shall set me up upon a rock.

Amen • thank you Jesus, Yes. Ebd

Thank Father for this new day, as I go forward, give your blessing and wisdom, please have your Angels go before, beyond, behind, above, beneath, and all around me, protecting me, my children, grandchildren, grate grandchildren, true family members and true friends from all seen and unsee events and dangers and all suffering, situations that not in your will cover me In your Anointed, power, going out, and coming in. Not my will, but your will be done on earth as it is in haven, in Jesus name I pray Amen

ebd

Daniel 4:26

"And whereas they commanded to leave the stump of the tree roots; thy kingdom shall be sure unto thee, after that thou shalt have known that the heavens do rule."

King James Version (KJV)

< > ▲ View Chapter

Daniel 4:26 Context

23And whereas the king saw a watcher and an holy one coming down from heaven, and saying, Hew the tree down, and destroy it; yet leave the stump of the roots thereof in the earth, even with a band of iron and brass, in the tender grass of the field; and let it be wet with the dew of heaven, and let his portion be with the beasts of the field, till seven times pass over him; 24This is the interpretation, 0 king, and this is the decree of the most High, which is come upon my lord the king: 25That they shall drive thee from men, and thy dwelling shall be with the beasts of the field, and they shall make thee to eat grass as oxen, and they shall wet thee with the dew of heaven, and seven times shall pass over thee, till thou know that the most High ruleth in the kingdom of men, and giveth it to whomsoever he will. 26And whereas they commanded to leave the stump of the tree roots; thy kingdom shall be sure unto thee, after that thou shalt have known that the heavens do rule. 27Wherefore, 0 king, let my counsel be acceptable unto thee, and break off thy sins by righteousness, and thine iniquities by shewing mercy to the poor; if it may be a lengthening of thy tranquillity. 28All this came upon the king Nebuchadnezzar. 29At the end of twelve months he walked in the palace of the kingdom of Babylon.

Isaiah 45:9

"Woe unto him that striveth with his Maker! Let the potsherd strive with the potsherds of the earth. Shall the clay say to him that fashioneth it, What makest thou? or thy work, He hath no hands?"

King James Version (KJV)

< > ▲ View Chapter

Isaiah 45:9 Context

6That they may know from the rising of the sun, and from the west, that there is none beside me. I am the LORD, and there is none else. 7I form the light, and create darkness: I make peace, and create evil: I the LORD do all these things. 8Drop down, ye heavens, from above, and let the skies pour down righteousness: let the earth open, and let them bring forth salvation, and let righteousness spring up together; I the LORD have created it. 9Woe unto him that striveth with his Maker! Let the potsherd strive with the potsherds of the earth. Shall the clay say to him that fashioneth it, What makest thou? or thy work, He hath no hands? 10Woe unto him that saith unto his father, What begettest thou? or to the woman, What hast thou brought forth? 11Thus saith the LORD, the Holy One of Israel, and his Maker, Ask me of things to come concerning my sons, and concerning the work of my hands command ye me. 12I have made the earth, and created man upon it: I, even my hands, have stretched out the heavens, and all their host have I commanded. Amen ,, thank you Jesus.ebd

"With good will doing service, as to the lord, and not to men:" Ephesians 6:7 KJV Amen yes, God thank you for your teaching and the wisdom, knowledge understanding you entrusted me with and showing me how to use it wisely Amen thank you Jesus. Yes, Lord, have your way in my life. Ebd

Daniel 5:11

"There is a man in thy kingdom, in whom is the spirit of the holy gods; and in the days of thy father light and understanding and wisdom, like the wisdom of the gods, was found in him; whom the king Nebuchadnezzar thy father, the king, I say, thy father, made master of the magicians, astrologers, Chaldeans, and soothsayers;"

King James Version {KJV)

< > ▲ View Chapter

Daniel 5:11 Context

8Then came in all the king's wise men: but they could not read the writing, nor make known to the king the interpretation thereof. 9Then was king Belshazzar greatly troubled, and his countenance was changed in him, and his lords were astonied. 10Now the queen, by reason of the words of the king and his lords, came into the banquet house: and the queen spake and said, O king, live forever: let not thy thoughts trouble thee, nor let thy countenance be changed: 11There is a man in thy kingdom, in whom is the spirit of the holy gods; and in the days of thy father light and understanding and wisdom, like the wisdom of the gods, was found in him; whom the king Nebuchadnezzar thy father, the king, I say, thy father, made master of the magicians, astrologers, Chaldeans, and soothsayers; 12Forasmuch as an excellent spirit, and knowledge, and understanding, interpreting of dreams, and shewing of hard sentences, and dissolving of doubts, were found in the same Daniel, whom the king named Belteshazzar: now let Daniel be called, and he will shew the interpretation. 13Then was Daniel brought in before the king. And the king spake and said unto Daniel, Art thou that Daniel, which art of the children of the captivity of Judah, whom the king my father brought out of Jewry? 14I have even heard of thee, that the spirit of the gods is in thee, and that light and understanding and excellent wisdom is found in thee. Amen yes God have your way ebd

Psalms 112: 1

"Praise ye the LORD. Blessed is the man that feareth the LORD, that delighteth greatly in his commandments."

King James Version (KN)

< > ▲ View Chapter

Psalms 112:1 Context

I Praise ye the LORD. Blessed is the man that feareth the LORD, that delighteth greatly in his commandments. 2His seed shall be mighty upon earth: the generation of the upright shall be blessed. 3Wealth and riches shall be in his house: and his righteousness endureth forever. 4Unto the upright there ariseth light in the darkness: he is gracious, and full of compassion, and righteous.

Amen ebd thank you Father for all of your blessings, and protection from all evil and danger seen and unseen, thank you for opening doors that only you can open, thank you for giving your Angels charge to watch over me both day and night, guiding my every movement, thank you Father and continue to cover me, my children, grandchildren and grate grandchildren in your in your arms and protection, in your Anointed prayers and power, in Jesus name I pray, giving you all Honor, and praise Amen. Ebd

And it shall come to pass, if thou shalt hearken diligently unto the voice of the LORD thy God, to observe and to do all his commandments which I command thee this day, that the LORD thy God will set thee on high above all nations of the earth:" Deuteronomy 28:1 KN

Yes Lord, thank you Jesus

And it shall come to pass, if thou shalt hearken diligently unto the voice of the LORD thy God, to observe and to do all his commandments which I command thee this day, that the LORD thy God will set thee on high above all nations of the earth:" Deuteronomy 28:1 KJV

Yes Lord, Thank you Jesus.

Thank you dear God for bringing us all through this week, as we continue forward into this wonderful blessed weekend, please continue to send your Angels to guide, lead and protect us all from all enemies, including those who may not have our best intentions in mind and heart. In Jesus name I have prayed God, I thank you.

Walking in faithfulness, not by
what I can see always keeping
God First Daily
Yes God I thank you.

Devil, you have no power here, I rebuke you by the power of the Holy Ghost, in the Blood of Jesus, I command you to return to sender, in Jesus name, Go, Go,Go! You have no power here by the blood of Jesus, Psalm91232737Is4717

ebd

Psalms 121:1

"(A Song of degrees.) I will lift up mine eyes unto the hills, from whence cometh my help."

King James Version (KJV)

< > ▲ View Chapter

Psalms 121: 1 Context

1(A Song of degrees.) I will lift up mine eyes unto the hills, from whence cometh my help. 2My help cometh from the LORD, which made heaven and earth. 3He will not suffer thy foot to be moved: he that keepeth thee will not slumber. 4Behold, he that keepeth Israel shall neither Ame thank you Jesus

Thank you Father for this new day, as I go forward gives you Angels charge to keep me safe from all evil and dangerous, seen and unseen situations, cover me under your wings of protection, bless me coming in, and bless me going out, continue to connect me with all the right people for all the right reasons, in Jesus name I pray, • ebd

Daniel 5:27

"TEKEL; Thou art weighed in the balances, and art found wanting."

King James Version (KN)

< > ▲ View Chapter

Daniel 5 :27 Context

24Then was the part of the hand sent from him; and this writing was written. 25And this is the writing that was written, MENE, MENE, TEKEL, UPHARSIN. 26This is the interpretation of the thing: MENE; God hath numbered thy kingdom, and finished it. 27TEKEL; Thou a11 weighed in the balances, and art found wanting. 28PERES; Thy kingdom is divided, and given to the Medes and Persians. 29Then commanded Belshazzar, and they clothed Daniel with scarlet, and put a chain of gold about his neck, and made a proclamation concerning him, that he should be the third ruler in the kingdom. 301n that night was Belshazzar the king of the Chaldeans slain. ebd

thank you Jesus

Thank you father for the new week as I go forward, please continue to guide and lead my path way in your will and your way, bless me going out and coming in in Jesus name. Continue to give your angels charge to watch over me my children, grandchildren, great grandchildren,true friends, and family members; protect us from all seen and unseen evil, and dangerous situation, and all those that do not have our best interest and intentions in their hearts and minds, thank you for you ordain anointing power of wisdom, knowledge, and understanding, favor, grace and mercy in Jesus name I pray amen. Yes Lord, thank you Jesus.ebd.

Devil, you have no power here, I rebuke you by the power of the Holy Ghost, in the Blood of Jesus, I command you to teturm to sender, in Jesus name, Go, Go,Go! You have no power here by the blood of Jesus, Psalm912327371s4717

Ecclesiastes 2:5

"I made me gardens and orchards, and I planted trees in them of all kind of fruits:"

King James Version (KJV)

< > ▲ View Chapter

Ecclesiastes 2:5 Context

21 said of laughter, It is mad: and of mirth, What doeth it? 31 sought in mine heart to give myself unto wine, yet acquainting mine heart with wisdom; and to lay hold on folly, till I might see what was that good for the sons of men, which they should do under the heaven all the days of their life. 41 made me great works; I builded me houses; I planted me vineyards: 51 made me gardens and orchards, and I planted trees in them of all kind of fruits: 61 made me pools of water, to water therewith the wood that bringeth forth trees: 71 got me servants and maidens, and had servants born in my house; also I had great possessions of great and small cattle above all that were in Jerusalem before me: 81 gathered me also silver and gold, and the peculiar treasure of kings and of the provinces: I gat me men singers and women singers, and the delights of the sons of men, as musical instruments, and that of all sorts.

Lord I thank you for this new day, for watching over us all as we all slept, and keeping us safe, waking us up in our right mindset, health and strength,, lord as we go forward in this beautiful day, continue to guide, lead, deliver, bless healing, our hearts, body, minds, and souls, order our footsteps, coming, and going, continue to connected us with all the right people for all the right reasons, and purposes, keeping us safe from all evil, and all those who may have evil intentions, toward us in their hearts and minds. In Jesus name I have prayed, yes God, send your Anointing, and your blessing, give your Angels charge to keep our children, grandchildren, and grate grandchildren safe from all evil spirits, and protect them in your your loving care, please protect and provide for all of us, keep us all safe under your loving wings, in your care. Amen, Amen thank you Jesus, yes God I am thankful to you daily for all of your many blessings, from the smallest, to the largest, I give you all Honor and praise.

1 Samuel 1:11

"And she vowed a vow, and said, 0 LORD of hosts, if thou wilt indeed look on the affliction of thine handmaid, and remember me, and not forget thine handmaid, but wilt give unto thine handmaid a man child, then I will give him unto the LORD all the days of his life, and there shall no razor come upon his head."

King James Version (KN)

< > ▲ View Chapter

1 Samuel 1 : 11 Context

8Then said Elkanah her husband to her, Hannah, why weepest thou? and why eatest thou not? and why is thy heart grieved? am not I better to thee than ten sons? 9So Hannah rose up after they had eaten in Shiloh, and after they had drunk. Now Eli the priest sat upon a seat by a post of the temple of the LORD. 10And she was in bitterness of soul, and prayed unto the LORD, and wept sore. 11And she vowed a vow, and said, O LORD of hosts, if thou wilt indeed look on the affliction of thine handmaid, and remember me, and not forget thine handmaid, but wilt give unto thine handmaid a man child, then I will give him unto the LORD all the days of his life, and there shall no razor come upon his head. 12And it came to pass, as she continued praying before the LORD, that Eli marked her mouth. 13Now Hannah, she spake in her heart; only her lips moved, but her voice was not heard: therefore Eli thought she had been drunken. 14And Eli said unto her, How long wilt thou be drunken? put away thy wine from thee.

Amen yes Lord, thank you Jesus.

WE HELP YOU WALK BETTER, AND RUN
FASTER, STEP- BY- STEP, KNOWING THAT
WITH GOD ALL THINGS ARE POSSIBLE,

Faith makes them possible,

Everything is moving, in and by the power of God!!

No weapon that is formed against thee shall prosper; and every tongue that shall rise against thee in judgment thou shalt condemn. This is the heritage of the servants of the LORD, and their righteousness is of me, saith the LORD." Isaiah 54:17 KJV

Thank you Jesus, yes, God, thank you Jesus.

Thank you dear God for this new day, continue to guide and lead our journey in your will and your way, providing and protecting our every movement, and steps, in your path of salvation, and wisdom In Jesus name I have prayed. Thank you God.

Teach your sons that cooking
and cleaning are basic life
skills not gender roles.

Thank you dear God for the wisdom, knowledge, and understanding, you have entrusted me with and showing me how to use it wisely, daily. thank you Father.

.

Stay Motivational &
Inspirational
My God is to be Much Better
than I was in the Pass, Not to
be better than Anyone Else.

Stay Motivated.
Life keep changing Everyday,
Nothing Stays the Same,
Never Stop Learning and
Keeping.
God First Everyday Always.

Deuteronomy 7:7

"The LORD did not set his love upon you, nor choose you, because ye were more in number than any people; for ye were the fewest of all people:"

King James Version (KJV)

< > ▲ View Chapter

Deuteronomy 7:7 Context

4For they will turn away thy son from following me, that they may serve other gods: so will the anger of the LORD be kindled against you, and destroy thee suddenly. 5But thus shall ye deal with them; ye shall destroy their altars, and break down their images, and cut down their groves, and burn their graven images with fire. 6For thou art an holy people unto the LORD thy God: the LORD thy God hath chosen thee to be a special people unto himself, above all people that are upon the face of the earth. 7The LORD did not set his love upon you, nor choose you, because ye were more in number than any people; for ye were the fewest of all people: 8But because the LORD loved you, and because he would keep the oath which he had sworn unto your fathers, hath the LORD brought you out with a mighty hand, and redeemed you out of the house of bondmen, from the hand of Pharaoh king of Egypt 9Know therefore that the LORD thy God, he is God, the faithful God, which keepeth covenant and mercy with them that love him and keep his commandments to a thousand generations; 1 0And repayeth them that hate him to their face, to destroy them: he will not be slack to him that hateth him, he will repay him to his face.

Copy Print Similar Verses

Amen thank you God.

In Jesus mighty name, Yes God, I am always Thankful daily In Jesus mighty name.

Good morning y'all,

Thank you dear God for all of your many blessings, thank you for watching over me and my family all night long as we sleep, protecting us all from all from of evil spirits, suffering, sickness, death, situations, and all forms of destruction, and danger, We all thank you in Jesus mighty name. Please continue to keep us all in your prayers, and protect us underneath your wings of protection, from all those who seek to do evil toward us, including those whom are pretending to be our friends, but in their hearts, they are fighting against us, trying to block our blessings, Father God Return their evil deeds back to all of our evil enemies. Backfire! Their evil deeds to destroy themselves. In Jesus name I have prayed, yes God I thank you please send your Angels of protection to fight, for me, no weapon formed against me, my children or my true family or friends, shall ever prosper.

In Jesus name .

Yes God, thank you Jesus

Inspirational
Learn from your past,
live for today, Have a
vision for your future.

Motivational
Saying "I Do" To our True
love ones only takes a second,
But the moment we say "I Do"
Stays In our Hearts Forever.

Everyday is a new beginning,
given by God, we can't
change yesterday we learned
from yesterday in hopes
of making a difference.

When God is in the Building,
Blessings unfolds and flows.
Yes, God I am thankful Daily.

Inspirational
Slow Start, Excellent Finish.
Never Look down on anyone
who is continually making
progress rather small or
large, or how slow they are
advancing. One day that
individual is going to make
it to the finish line in Life.

Motivational
Happiness doesn't have to be
about you getting Everything
you want in Life.
Happiness is about being
thankful and enjoying all
God have bless you with
daily. A smile, good health,
hands, feet, a home, car, etc.

Father, you don't see me like I am, you see me like I'm going to be, I thank you Yes, Father I am thankful.

With God all things are possible, only have faith trust God and believe.

Psalms 54:6

"I will freely sacrifice unto thee: I will praise thy name, 0 LORD; for it is good."

King James Version (KJV)

< > ▲ View Chapter

Psalms 54:6 Context

3For strangers are risen up against me, and oppressors seek after my soul: they have not set God before them. Selah. 4Behold, God is mine helper: the Lord is with them that uphold my soul. 5He shall reward evil unto mine enemies: cut them off in thy truth. 61 will freely sacrifice unto thee: I will praise thy name, 0 LORD; for it is good. 7For he hath delivered me out of all trouble: and mine eye hath seen his desire upon mine enemies.

Amen in Jesus mighty name, I am thankful, daily; yes God our Father.

Thank you dear God for this blessed day, as I go forward into this new day, Lead and guide my entire journey through every step of the journey that has been set before me, opening doors, closing doors, and putting me in your path of success, righteousness, prosperity and happiness, all the Fruits of your spirit. Cover me underneath your wings, of protection, keeping me safe from all evil spirits, evil people, all demons, and all danger. Thank you for your Holy Ghost, Delivance, and all of your many blessings, both large, and small. I'm thankful daily. In Jesus name I have prayed.

Father, send your Angels and your Anointed power. 'Yes Work it out, No weapon formed against me, my children, shall ever prosper, In Jesus name.

Numbers 7:24

"On the third day Eliab the son of Helon, prince of the children of Zebulun, did offer:"

King James Version (KJV)

< > ▲ View Chapter

Numbers 7:24 Context

21 One young bullock, one ram, one lamb of the first year, for a burnt offering: 22One kid of the goats for a sin offering: 23And for a sacrifice of peace offerings, two oxen, five rams, five he goats, five lambs of the first year: this was the offering of Nethaneel the son of Zuar. 24On the third day Eliab the son of Helon, prince of the children of Zebulun, did offer: 25His offering was one silver charger, the weight whereof was an hundred and thirty shekels, one silver bowl of seventy shekels, after the shekel of the sanctuary; both of them full of fine flour mingled with oil for a meat offering: 26One golden spoon of ten shekels, full of incense: 27One young bullock, one ram, one lamb of the first year, for a burnt offering:

Amen Thank you Jesus, yes.

Thank you dear God for this new day and new week, I thank you for bringing all of us safely through the weekend, as we forward in our daily routine, please continue to watch over us all, especially those who are exposed to outside influences of the community, weather conditions, of extreme heat keep us safe in all our homes, please give your Angels charge to guide our every movement, in your Anointing power, covering all of us underneath your power of prayer and protection keep all our children safe in your care, In Jesus name I have prayed, yes God I thank you For all of your many blessings, from the smallest to the largest, we give you all praises, and all Honors send your Anointing In Jesus mighty name, God.

Kindness is like snow.
It beautifies
everything it covers.
Kahlil Gibran

"But because the LORD loved you, and because he would keep the oath which he had sworn unto your fathers, hath the LORD brought you out with a mighty hand, and redeemed you out of the house of bondmen, from the hand of Pharaoh king of Egypt." Deuteronomy 7:8 KJV

Amen thank you Jesus, Yes Lord.

Thank, Dear God for this new day and new beginning. Yes God I am thankful to you.

Good morning y'all,

Thank you dear God for this day, as I go forward into this new day of new beginnings, order my footsteps, mind, body, heart, soul, and blessings me in all aspects of my life. According to your will and your way, covering us in your presence, and protecting us from all evil, and danger, all this whom don't have my best interest in mind, and wishing to do me evil. Backfire, to them, ln Jesus mighty name, I have prayed. Yes God, send your Angels of referral Anointing, O placed everything in your hand you fight against all those who fight against me .No, weapons formed against me shall proposer.

The Joy of the Lord is
my strength. Yes God
I am Thankful Daily.

Good morning y'all,

Father as we come before you this morning, not to ask for anything, but to say thank you, for all the wonderful things that you've given us all on a daily basis, from the smallest things to the largest things, we thank you for clean air, water, food, clothes, home, health, car bed jobs, our family, friends, and all the things that we have not seen, provided for us, protecting us as we go on our daily journey, you are always there protecting us, Father, we all says thank you, for everything. In Jesus name I have prayed. Yes God, we thank you, Amen.

Isaiah 56:3

"Neither let the son of the stranger, that hath joined himself to the LORD, speak, saying, The LORD hath utterly separated me from his people: neither let the eunuch say, Behold, I am a dry tree."

King James Version (KJV)

< > ▲ View Chapter

Isaiah 56:3 Context

1Thus saith the LORD, Keep ye judgment, and do justice: for my salvation is near to come, and my righteousness to be revealed. 2Blessed is the man that doeth this, and the son of man that layeth hold on it; that keepeth the sabbath from polluting it, and keepeth his hand from doing any evil. 3Neither let the son of the stranger, that hath joined himself to the LORD, speak, saying, The LORD hath utterly separated me from his people: neither let the eunuch say, Behold, I am a dry tree. 4For thus saith the LORD unto the eunuchs that keep my sabbaths, and choose the things that please me, and take hold of my covenant; 5Even unto them will I give in mine house and within my walls a place and a name better than of sons and of daughters: I will give them an everlasting name, that shall not be cut off. 6Alsb the sons of the stranger, that join themselves to the LORD, to serve him, and to love the name of the LORD, to be his servants, every one that keepeth the sabbath from polluting it, and taketh hold of my covenant; Amen yes God, I thank you.

Thank you dear God for this day, please continue to send your Angels to guide, lead and protect me, my children, family members, friends. From all forms of evil, and danger, all those that do not have my beBt interest in their hearts and minds. Amen in Jesus mighty name, I have prayed.

With god, all things are possible, only have faith, trust God and believe.

Daniel 5:26

"This is the interpretation of the thing: MENE; God hath numbered thy kingdom, and finished it."

King James Version (KN)

< > ▲ View Chapter

Daniel 5:26 Context

23B ut hast lifted up thyself against the Lord of heaven; and they have brought the vessels of his house before thee, and thou, and thy lords, thy wives, and thy concubines, have drunk wine in them; and thou hast praised the gods of silver, and gold, of brass, iron, wood, and stone, which see not, nor hear, nor know: and the God in whose hand thy breath is, and whose are all thy ways, hast thou not glorified: 24Then was the part of the hand sent from him; and this writing was written. 25And this is the writing that was written, MENE, MENE, TEKEL, UPHARSIN. 26This is the interpretation of the thing: MENE; God hath numbered thy kingdom, and finished it. 27TEKEL; Thou art weighed in the balances, and art found wanting. 28PERES; Thy kingdom is divided, and given to the Medes and Persians. 29Then commanded Belshazzar, and they clothed Daniel with scarlet, and put a chain of gold about his neck, and made a proclamation concerning him, that he should be the third ruler in the kingdom. Amen •• thank you Jesus.yes Lord ebd

Thank you Father for this blessing of a new day, Amen,

to be a part of and to be a blessing to others, as we go forward in Jesus name, have me to pray fasting and guide me in your path with grace and mercy, and love, in still in me as I journey forward the faith and the fruits, of your spirit, thank you for all of the many blessings you have given me and for all the blessings to continue in my journey forward according to your plan and your will, and your way, in Grace, in Jesus name. Father, thank you for choosing me and continue covering me In your Anointed Faith, peace love, mercy, prosperity, protection, forgiveness, healing, health, happiness, and porcting, me, my children, grandchildren, grate grandchildren, true friends and family members, from all from of evil, danger, Amen ebd

Walking in the light shinning all around me all day and night. Yes Lord thank you Jesus thank you. you are my Guiding light ebd.

Holy Ghost
you're Welcome here!
Yes God.

Have a safe and
blessed week, everyone!
Always keep God first daily.

Nothing can stop God's
plan for your life.

Thank you dear God, for bringing us all through the week and into this weekend, as we go forward with this new week continue to send your Angels to guid lead and protect use from all dangers and evils both, seen and unseen. Cover, cover us all in your Anointed power and strength, delivering us from all enemies in Jesus name I have prayed, yes & God I thank you Jesus. Amen.

Thank you dear God for giving us this day, as we go forward into this week with thanks given, send your Angels before, beside, behind, beneath, above beyond, and all around us protecting us from all seen and unseen, evils and dangers, and all those that don't have our best interest in their eyes, hearts, and minds. In Jesus name I have prayed, yes & God, I give you all Honor, Glory, and praise, thank you Jesus, send your Angels of Mercy and cover me in your Anointing and power of the Holy Ghost, keep my heart, mind, spirit, and soul in your righteous spirit all the time, away from all evil spirits that is not your Holy spiritual presence and Anointing. yes, Lord to your will and your way

Thank you dear God, for bringing us all through the week and into this weekend, as we go forward with this new week continue to send your Angels to guid lead and protect use from all dangers and evils both, seen and unseen. Cover,cover us all in your Anointed power and strength, delivering us from all enemies in Jesus name I have prayed, yes God I thank you Jesus. Amen.

Matt:22: 37-46

37. Jesus said unto him, Thou shalt love the Lord thy God with all thy heart, and with all thy soul, and with all thy mind.

38. This is the first and great commandment.

39. And the second is like unto it, Thou shalt love thy neighbor as thyself.

40. On these two commandments hang all the law and the prophets.

41. While the Pharisees were gathered together, Jesus asked them,

42. Saying, What think ye of Christ? whose son is he? They say unto him, The Son of David.

43. He saith unto them, How then doth David in spirit call him Lord, saying,

44. The LORD said unto my Lord, Sit thou on my right hand, till I make37 thine enemies thy footstool?

45. If David then call him Lord, how is he his son?

46. And no man was able to answer him a word, neither durst any man from that day forth ask him any more questions.

Amen, yes Lord, thank you Jesus.

Chapter 1

Bible Options

1 The former treatise have I made, 0 Theophilus, of all that Jesus began both to do and teach,

2 Until the day in which he was taken up, after that he through the Holy Ghost had given commandments unto the apostles whom he had chosen:

3 To whom also he shewed himself alive after his passion by many infallible proofs, being seen of them forty days, and speaking of the things pertaining to the kingdom of God:

4 And, being assembled together with them, commanded them that they should not depart from Jerusalem, but wait for the promise of the Father, which, saith he, ye have heard of me. 5 For John truly baptized with water; but ye shall be baptized with the Holy Ghost not many days hence.

6 When they therefore were come together, they asked of him, saying, Lord, wilt thou at this time restore again the kingdom to Israel?

7 And he said unto them, It is not for you to know the times or the seasons, which the Father hath put in his own power.

8 But ye shall receive power, after that the Holy Ghost

is come upon you: and ye shall be witnesses unto me both in Jerusalem, and in all Judaea, and in Samaria, and unto the uttermost part of the earth.

9 And when he had spoken these things, while they beheld, he was taken up; and a cloud received him out of their sight.

10 And while they looked stedfastly toward heaven as he went up, behold, two men stood by them in white apparel;

11 Which also said, Ye men of Galilee, why stand ye gazing up into heaven? this same Jesus, which is taken up from you into heaven, shall so come in like manner as ye have seen him go into heaven.

12 Then returned they unto Jerusalem from the mount called Olivet, which is from Jerusalem a sabbath day's journey.

13 And when they were come in, they went up into an upper room, where abode both Peter, and James, and John, and Andrew, Philip, and Thomas, Bartholomew, and Matthew, James the son of Alphaeus, and Simon Zelotes, and Judas the brother of James.

Kindness, compassion,
love and respect for self
and others pass it forward.
In Jesus mighty name.

I am glad they said unto me Let us go into the house of the Lord In Jesus name, For my house is a house of prayer for all people., As for me and my house we will serve the Lord, Father send your Anointing, Ordained Holy Ghost, and power, Let it In Jesus name. Yes God I thank you. For all of your many blessings, and blessings to come, N, S, E, W. All sides, both seen and unseen. in Jesus Name.

Psalms 49:1

"(To the chief Musician, A Psalm for the sons of Korah.) Hear this, all ye people; give ear, all ye inhabitants of the world:"

King James Version (KJV)

< > ▲ View Chapter

Psalms 49:1 Context

1 (To the chief Musician, A Psalm for the sons of Korah.) Hear this, all ye people; give ear, all ye inhabitants of the world: 2Both low and high, rich and poor, together. 3My mouth shall speak of wisdom; and the meditation of my heart shall be of understanding. 4I will incline mine ear to a parable: I will open my dark saying upon the harp.

Amen in Jesus name.

Thank you Dear God for this new day, as I go forward into this day, give your Angels charge

to go before me, to guide my every move and footsteps, protecting the me from all forms of evil and danger and all those who don't have my best interest in their heart and mind, continue to cover me, my children family in your Anointing, In Jesus name I have prayed, yes God thank you Jesus.

Thank you dear God for watching over me all night long, waking me up in my right mind health and strength, protecting us all from all see and unseen dangers and evil, creating in us all a right mindset and a clean heart, fill with your love and compassion. Kindness, , Grace, peace, and mercy, and respect for others and ourselves, covers us under your watchful eyes, protecting us from all dangers situations, including those that may arise out of jealousy, hatred from those that don't have our best interests, and intentions in their hearts and minds, keep me in your care, in your Anointed power, and your faith, your ways and your will, not my will but, your will, protect our children, grandchildren, grate grandchildren, from all suffering, seen, and unseen, danger, evil, all that don't have their best interests, in mind, and heart. Ordained your Angels of Grace, Peace, Love, mercy, wisdom, knowledge, compassion, kindness, to abide, with all of us daily. In Jesus name I have prayed. Thank you God.

Psalms 1:1

"Blessed is the man that walketh not in the counsel of the ungodly, nor standeth in the way of sinners, nor sitteth in the seat of the scornful."

King James Version (KJV)

< > ▲ View Chapter

Psalms 1:1 Context

1 Blessed is the man that walketh not in the counsel of the ungodly, nor standeth in the way of sinners, nor sitteth in the seat of the scornful. 2But his delight is in the law of the LORD; and in his law doth he meditate day and night. 3And he shall be like a tree planted by the rivers of water, that bringeth forth his fruit in his season; his leaf also shall not wither; and whatsoever he doeth shall prosper. 4The ungodly are not so: but are like the chaff which the wind driveth away. Amen

Titus 2:11

"For the grace of God that bringeth salvation hath appeared to all men,"

King James Version (KJV)

< > ▲ View Chapter

Titus 2: 11 Context

8Sound speech, that cannot be condemned; that he that is of the contrary part may be ashamed, having no evil thing to say of you. 9Exhort servants to be obedient unto their own masters, and to please them well in all things; not answering again; 10Not purloining, but shewing all good fidelity; that they may adorn the doctrine of God our Saviour in all things. 11 For the grace of God that bringeth salvation hath appeared to all men, 12Teaching us that, denying ungodliness and worldly lusts, we should live soberly, righteously, and godly, in this present world; 13Looking for that blessed hope, and the glorious appearing of the great God and our Saviour Jesus Christ; 14Who gave himself for us, that he might redeem us from all iniquity, and purify unto himself a peculiar people, zealous of good works. Amen Thank you Jesus yes God.

Thank your Lord for this opportunity to serve you in the beauty of Holiness today, tomorrow, and going forward in Jesus name in the future in faith, love, peace, grace and mercy, wisdom, knowledge, understanding, compassion, courage, prayer continue protecting, prosperous, prosperity, health, happiness, comfort, covered in the glory, prosperity, strength, safety, spiritual strength in the Anointing positive spirit, of light walking and living on God, Grace, abundance's officials, Devine teacher. And choose vesual

Continue to charge your Anointed powerful Angels to guide, lead, provide, support, protect, me, my children, grandchildren, grate grandchildren, true, faithful Family Members, and friends. In Jesus name, I have prayed.

Deuteronomy 6:15

"(For the LORD thy God is a jealous God among you) lest the anger of the LORD thy God be kindled against thee, and destroy thee from off the face of the earth."

King James Version (KJV

< > ▲ View Chapter

Deuteronomy 6:15 Context

12Then beware lest thou forget the LORD, which brought thee forth out of the land of Egypt, from the house of bondage. 13Thou shalt fear the LORD thy God, and serve him, and shalt swear by his name. 14Ye shall not go after other gods, of the gods of the people which are round about you; 15(For the LORD thy God is a jealous God among you) lest the anger of the LORD thy God be kindled against thee, and destroy thee from off the face of the earth. 16Ye shall not tempt the LORD your God, as ye tempted him in Massah. 17Ye shall diligently keep the commandments of the LORD your God, and his testimonies, and his statutes, which he hath commanded thee. 18And thou shalt do that which is right and good in the sight of the LORD: that it may be well with thee, and that thou mayest go in and possess the good land which the LORD sware unto thy fathers,

Amen Thank you Jesus

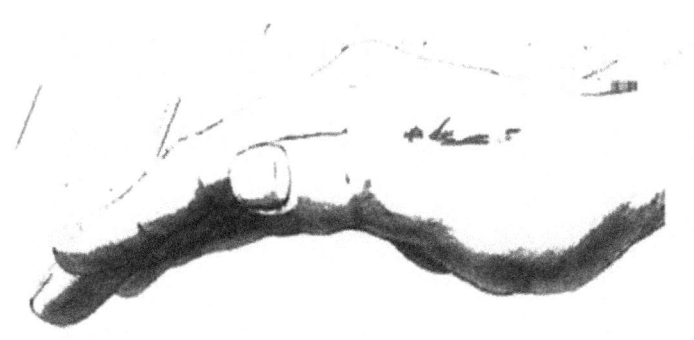

God will never leave you
alone. No matter what
situation you are facing,
God is with you.
Touch here & insert Amen

Psalms 117:1

"O praise the LORD, all ye nations: praise him, all ye people."

King James Version (KJV)

< > ▲ View Chapter

Psalms 117:1 Context

10 praise the LORD, all ye nations: praise him, all ye people. 2For his merciful kindness is great toward us: and the truth of the LORD endureth forever. Praise ye the LORD. Amen Amen, Amen Thank you Jesus, yes Lord, Have your way.

Thank you Father for this amazing opportunity to share this beautiful new day, in Jesus name, thank you for giving your Angels charge to keep us safe from all evil spirits, and danger, for delivering me from all evil minds of those that don't have my best interest, and intentions in their heart, mind, and soul. Thank you Father for making away, for me, my children, grandchildren, grate grandchildren, true family members and friends, thank you for all of the many blessings you have given us, from the smallest to the largest, thank you for strengthening us, guiding and leading, helping, protecting, understanding us and defending, delivering, and supporting, providing, and speaking to us, supporting, and fighting our battles, for all our lives, thank you •• for faithfulness, wisdom, knowledge, kindness, compassion, faith, love, prayer, peace, gratitude, grace, and mercy, and prosperity, thank you Father for showing me how to take what you have given me, understanding and uplifting, using it wisely and giving you all Honor and Praise, and Glory, thank you for choosing and continuing to cover me in your prayers, and Anointing positive light , and power .in Jesus Name I have prayed. Amen Amen, Amen. Thank you Jesus, Lord have your way. Work it out thank you for everything, establishing my gratitude going forward, as I am going in, and coming out, with all the right people for all the right reasons and righteousness purposes.

Psalms 40:6

"Sacrifice and offering thou didst not desire; mine ears hast thou opened: burnt offering and sin offering hast thou not required."

King James Version (KJV)

< > ▲ View Chapter

Psalms 40:6 Context

3And he hath put a new song in my mouth, even praise unto our God: many shall see it, and fear, and shall trust in the LORD. 4Blessed is that man that maketh the LORD his trust, and respecteth not the proud, nor such as turn aside to lies. 5Many, 0 LORD my God, are thy wonderful works which thou hast done, and thy thoughts which are to us-ward: they cannot be reckoned up in order unto thee: if I would declare and speak of them, they are more than can be numbered. 6Sacrifice and offering thou didst not desire; mine ears hast thou opened: burnt offering and sin offering hast thou not required. 7Then said I, Lo, I come: in the volume of the book it is written of me, 81 delight to do thy will, 0 my God: yea, thy law is within my heart. 91 have preached righteousness in the great congregation: lo, I have not refrained my lips, O LORD, thou knowest. Amen Thank you Jesus I love you Lord.

Good morning everyone,

Thank you dear God for this blessed day and blessed Holy Week as we celebrate Christmas •

Holidays, keep us all safe, healthy and well, cover us in your Anointed Spirit, away from all

enemies, evil, and darkness and dangers, seen and unseen, in Jesus name I pray Amen thank you Jesus, yes God.

Daniel 1:4

"Children in whom was no blemish, but well favoured, and skilful in all wisdom, and cunning in knowledge, and understanding science, and such as had ability in them to stand in the king's palace, and whom they might teach the learning and the tongue of the Chaldeans."

King James Version (KJV)

< > ▲ View Chapter

Daniel 1 :4 Context

1In the third year of the reign of Jehoiakim king of Judah came Nebuchadnezzar king of Babylon unto Jerusalem, and besieged it. 2And the Lord gave Jehoiakim king of Judah into his hand, with part of the vessels of the house of God: which he carried into the land of Shinar to the house of his god; and he brought the vessels into the treasure house of his god. 3And the king spake unto Ashpenaz the master of his eunuchs, that he should bring certain of the children of Israel, and of the king's seed, and of the princes; 4Children in whom was no blemish, but well favoured, and skilful in all wisdom, and cunning in knowledge, and understanding science, and such as had ability in them to stand in the king's palace, and whom they might teach the learning and the tongue of the Chaldeans. 5And the king appointed them a daily provision of the king's meat, and of the wine which he drank: so nourishing them three years, that at the end thereof they might stand before the king. 6Now among these were of the children of Judah, Daniel, Hananiah, Mishael, and Azariah: 7Unto whom the prince of the eunuchs gave names: for he gave unto Daniel the name of Belteshazzar; and to Hananiah, of Shadrach; and to Mishael, of Meshach; and to Azariah, of Abednego.

Amen Amen Amen I love you lord, thank you Jesus.

Isaiah 56:4

"For thus saith the LORD unto the eunuchs that keep my sabbaths, and choose the things that please me, and take hold of my covenant;"

King James Version (KJV)

< > ▲ View Chapter

Isaiah 56:4 Context

1Thus saith the LORD, Keep ye judgment, and do justice: for my salvation is near to come, and my righteousness to be revealed. 2Blessed is the man that doeth this, and the son of man that layeth hold on it; that keepeth the sabbath from polluting it, and keepeth his hand from doing any evil. 3Neither let the son of the stranger, that hath joined himself to the LORD, speak, saying, The LORD hath utterly separated me from his people: neither let the eunuch say, Behold, I am a dry tree. 4For thus saith the LORD unto the eunuchs that keep my sabbaths, and choose the things that please me, and take hold of my covenant; 5Even unto them will I give in mine house and within my walls a place and a name better than of sons and of daughters: I will give them an everlasting name, that shall not be cut off. 6Also the sons of the stranger, that join themselves to the LORD, to serve him, and to love the name of the LORD, to be his servants, every one that keepeth the sabbath from polluting it, and taketh hold of my covenant; 7Even them will I bring to my holy mountain, and make them joyful in my house of prayer: their burnt offerings and their sacrifices shall be accepted upon mine altar; for mine house shall be called an house of prayer for all people.

Matthew 6:33

"But seek ye first the kingdom of God, and his righteousness; and all these things shall be added unto you."

King James Version (KJV)

< > ▲ View Chapter

Matthew 6:33 Context

30Wherefore, if God so clothe the grass of the field, which to day is, and to morrow is cast into the oven, shall he not much more clothe you, 0 ye of little faith? 31Therefore take no thought, saying, What shall we eat? or, What shall we drink? or, Wherewithal shall we be clothed? 32(For after all these things do the Gentiles seek:) for your heavenly Father knoweth that ye have need of all these things. 33But seek ye first the kingdom of God, and his righteousness; and all these things shall be added unto you. 34Take therefore no thought for the morrow: for the morrow shall take thought for the things of itself. Sufficient unto the day is the evil thereof. Amen thank you Jesus.

It's not what we may or may not have, it's how we use what God have blessed us with, with wisdom, Wisley. to help make a difference in our lives and the lives of others, pass it forward. (ebd)

Matthew 6:33

"But seek ye first the kingdom of God, and his righteousness; and all these things shall be added unto you."

King James Version (KJV)

< > ▲ View Chapter

Matthew 6:33 Context

30Wherefore, if God so clothe the grass of the field, which to day is, and to morrow is cast into the oven, shall he not much more clothe you, O ye of little faith? 31Therefore take no thought, saying, What shall we eat? or, What shall we drink? or, Wherewithal shall we be clothed? 32(For after all these things do the Gentiles seek:) for your heavenly Father knoweth that ye have need of all these things. 33But seek ye first the kingdom of God, and his righteousness; and all these things shall be added unto you. 34Take therefore no thought for the morrow: for the morrow shall take thought for the things of itself. Sufficient unto the day is the evil thereof. Amen thank you Jesus.

Richie Clarke:
Hello . How are doing? Your post are wonderful and interesting. We are not friends on Facebook and i would like us to be, but I don't want to intrude into your privacy by sending a request. I will appreciate if you can send me a friend request if you don't mind Thanks

Lester's Diabetic Consulting Service:
This Joy, Love, Peace, kindness, mercy, meekness, compassion, loyalty, Grace, long suffering, I have; the world give it to me only God, give it to me. Amen.

Lester's Diabetic Consulting Service:
Your building is your body, soul and sprite transformed by the renewing of your minds.

Lester's Diabetic Consulting Service:
When God is in the building, all souls are healed, thank you Father, for sending your Angles, charged with your Anointing, Armer of Grace, Love, Peace, and mercy, and healing. guiding all in your will and your way, with provision.

Good morning Everyone,

Have a wonderful blessed day In Jesus mighty, always keep God first daily, Amen, thank you Jesus.

Audrey Elaine Johnson:
Same to you beautiful

Grow Serenity:
It is found everywhere in our countryside, and we often ignore it, yet this plant could save a human being's life. Read full article in the first comment

Healthylifestyle:
Freeze Lemons: A Natural Remedy for Diabetes, Tumors, and Obesity That Will Amaze You! Must express something to keep getting my recipes .... Thank you

Full Recipe in First (c.o.m.m.e.n.t).

Healthylifestyle:
I'm 60 years old and this food has given me back my vision, removed fat from my liver and cleansed my colon only polite members will say thanks for the recipe Recipe in first comment.

Healthylifestyle:
Natural BOMB for cleansing the liver and blood vessels.

Only polite members say thank you.

Full recipe in the first comment

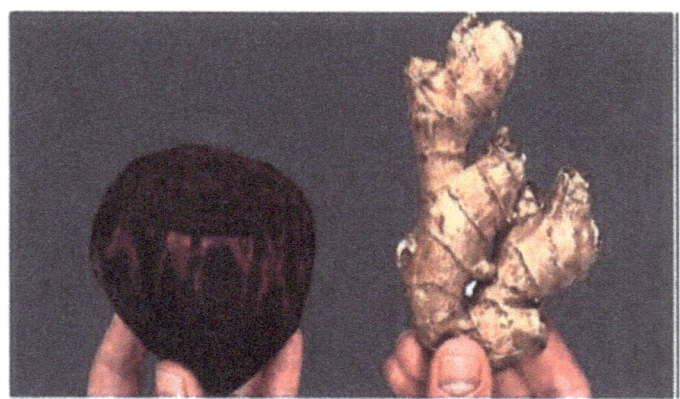

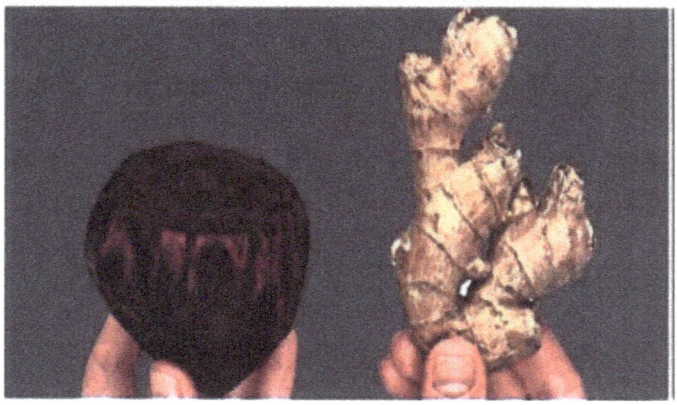

Motivational And Inspirational

Thankful Daily
By
Ethel
Brown
Dandy

Be goods to others

for NO reason.

It Costs Nothing to be kind to others you will only make others feel good and you will also feel better about yourself, as well.

We never know what others are going through. (EBD)

Being Beautiful

Being beautiful has Nothing
to do with how a person
may or may not look.

Being beautiful is how you make
others feel about themselves.

"Nothing Buit the Pure in heart shall see God."

Keep your intentions pure, you gain, they lose you Everything & Be positive pure in heart.

(ebd)

Make others feel welcome!

Making others feel welcome may open
up a whole new door for you as well
as making others to feel welcome,
valued, Love, and supported.

Kindness pass it forward
In Jesus Name. (ebd)

Talk with God In prayers

Talk with God in prayers about
all your problems. He cares
and will guide and lead you to
make the right decision.

He is closer than your best friends
some of them may not care, and some
of them may be glad to see and know
you are having problems." "(wisdom)"

(ebd)

Be a good Person

Never stop, being the
person God made you.

Because of bad people behaviors
toward you. (ebd)

Always be grateful to God,
with a positive thought and
have a grateful heart for God
at the end of everyday. (ebd)

Never discourage anyone who is trying an continually make progress, regardless by how slow their pace maybe.

They are still ahead of those that aren't trying.

AMEN.

Thank you Lord.

(ebd)

The Power of God!

God parted the red sea,

God didn't move the red sea,

God will fight all your battles,

God doesn't have to remove
the mountains,

God will make a way to take
you through the problems.
(mountains). Be bless

Peace Be Still!

(ebd)

Let Go,

Let God

Give it to God

God will give you back better
than what you give to him.

No matter what the situation is,
you maybe facing, keep the faith,
Knowing God have never lost a
case. Have faith believe in God.

"Yes God"! (ebd)

Put All Your Trust In God
He will direct your Path.

God will restore your health, heal
your wounds, turn sadness in to joy.

Put your trust in God.

(EBD)

Be Brave As A Lion.

Stand for what you know is right,
Stand for what you believe in.

Stand Lion!

Even if you must stand alone, God
is standing strong with you.

(EBD)

5 Rules for Love

1. Listen

2. Listen

3. Listen

4. Listen

5. Listen

It's a duty that never fails
God is watching. (ebd)

My hands may shake as

I prepare to Fight my battles

I am slaying demons,

I am a warrior

I am stronger than you realize.

God is fighting all my
battle along with me.

(EBD)

In life,

In old Age, we have a Lot of
Experience to share and Help
Everyone. Maybe a difference,

In Life

If everyone would ask
more questions. (ebd)

Inspire others with your story.

Don't be ashamed of your past.

Step out in faith.

God will meet us their wisdom. Ebd

Have Faith

And whatever you ask God for
In prayer you will receive.

I have faith and I believe In
Jesus mighty Name.

Amen

ebd

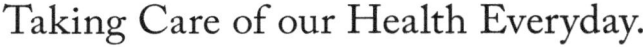

Taking Care of our Health Everyday.

A.D.L= Activity of Daily Living
A small things add up to Big things

1. Exercise
2. Eat Healthy
3. Take Time For yourself
4. Try New things
5. Connect with Family & Friends

Have a great quality of life daily.

(ebd)

Being Rich:

Being Rich is not what in a
person's Bank account,

But

Being Rich is what a person
Have in their Heart.

Out of the Heart How Rives of
wealth and compassion, Love
and Respect for others.

(ebd)

Happiness

Learning to appreciate what God has blessed us with, Everyday is the best Happiness we can experience. (ebd)

"The LORD shall command the blessing upon thee in thy storehouses, and in all that thou settest thine hand unto; and he shall bless thee in the land which the LORD thy God giveth thee." Deuteronomy 28:8

KJV

Amen, yes God, in Jesus mighty name.

Grandma's recipes:

Fried Cornbread - Southern Cornmeal Hoecakes

Ingredients

2/3 cup cornmeal

1/3 cup self rising flour

1/3 cup low fat buttermilk

1 large egg

oil for frying (I used about 3 tbsps coconut oil, but you can use whatever you like)

Instructions

Combine first 4 ingredients together in a bowl, mixing well. Mixture should be very moist but not soupy. Heat oil in skillet and drop by spoonfuls into oil. Cook til brown on one side and flip (it cooks kind of like a pancake) to brown on the other side. Place on plate with paper towels and blot any excess oil.

John 1 :5

"And the light shineth in darkness; and the darkness comprehended it not."

King James Version (KJV)

< > ▲ View Chapter

John 1 :5 Context

2The same was in the beginning with God. 3All things were made by him; and without him was not anything made that was made. 4In him was life; and the life was the light of men. 5And the light shineth in darkness; and the darkness comprehended it not. 6There was a man sent from God, whose name was John. 7The same came for a witness, to bear witness of the Light, that all men through him might believe. 8He was not that Light, but was sent to bear witness of that Light.

Lester's Diabetic Consulting Service:
When God Is in the plan, we don't see it, but God is working it out in our favor, to God Glory, yes Lord.

Psalms 104:4

"Who maketh his angels spirits; his ministers a flaming fire:"

King James Version (KJV)

< > ▲ View Chapter

Psalms 104:4 Context

1 Bless the LORD, 0 my soul. 0 LORD my God, thou art very great; thou art clothed with honour and majesty. 2Who coverest thyself with light as with a garment: who stretchest out the heavens like a curtain: 3Who layeth the beams of his chambers in the waters: who maketh the clouds his chariot: who walketh upon the wings of the wind: 4Who maketh his angels spirits; his ministers a flaming fire: 5Who laid the foundations of the earth, that it should not be removed for ever. 6Thou coveredst it with the deep as with a garment: the waters stood above the mountains. 7At thy rebuke they fled; at the voice of thy thunder they hasted away.

Amen Amen Thank you Jesus,Yes God.

Raising child is one of the hardest things we'll ever do, but loving them is the easiest we've ever done.

Slow progress

is better than no progress.

Stay positive and don't give up.

This Joy, Love, Peace, kindness, mercy, meekness, compassion, loyalty, Grace, long suffering, I have; the world didn't give it to me, only God, give it to me,

Amen.

Thank you Dear God for this new day and new beginning. YES God I am thankful to you.

Sometimes you need to let go of the picture of what you thought your life would be like and learn to find joy in the life you're living now, Lord am grateful.

Thank you dear God, for watching over us all night, and waking us up early in our right mind, health and strength, thank you for bringing all of us through the weekend and into this new week, thank you for all the wonderful blessings you have given to us, to enjoy and to give you all Honor and praise, thank you for your Amazing Grace, Mercy, love and support, and peace, thank you for everything you've given me in the past, presence and blessings to continue to come in the future. Thank you dear God for sending your Angels to protect, guide and lead us in your way of wisdom, knowledge and understanding. Thank you for putting us in contact with all the right people for all of the right reasons, and purposes. Thank you for keeping me, my children and grandchildren, great grandchildren, family and friends, safe under your wings of grace, love, peace, and prosperity, and protection. Thank the Lord, in Jesus name I have prayed. Yes, God I am thankful, to you daily for all of your many, blessings. In Jesus name I have prayed send your Angels and Anointing Power In Jesus name, to fight against evil, and danger, from all enemies, from the North, South, East, and west. no weapon formed against us all shall ever purposes. I thank you God. The battle is not ours, it's the Lord.

2 Chronicles 20:15

"And he said, Hearken ye, all Judah, and ye inhabitants of Jerusalem, and thou king Jehoshaphat, Thus saith the LORD unto you, Be not afraid nor dismayed by reason of this great multitude; for the battle is not yours, but God's."

King James Version (KJV)

< > ▲ View Chapter

2 Chronicles 20:15 Context

120 our God, wilt thou not judge them? for we have no might against this great company that cometh against us; neither know we what to do: but our eyes are upon thee. 13And all Judah stood before the LORD, with their little ones, their wives, and their children. 14Then upon Jahaziel the son of Zechariah, the son of Benaiah, the son of Jeiel, the son of Mattaniah, a Levite of the sons of Asaph, came the Spirit of the LORD in the midst of the congregation; 15And he said, Hearken ye, all Judah, and ye inhabitants of Jerusalem, and thou king Jehoshaphat, Thus saith the LORD unto you, Be not afraid nor dismayed by reason of this great multitude; for the battle is not yours, but God's. 16To morrow go ye down against them: behold, they come up by the cliff of Ziz; and ye shall find them at the end of the brook, before the wilderness of Jeruel. 17Ye shall not need to fight in this battle: set yourselves, stand ye still, and see the salvation of the LORD with you, O Judah and

Jerusalem: fear not, nor be dismayed; tomorrow go out against them: for the LORD will be with you. 18And Jehoshaphat bowed his head with his face to the ground: and all Judah and the inhabitants of Jerusalem fell before the LORD, worshipping the LORD.

Be wear Everyone, there
is a lot of fake pages have
popped up using my
picture and information,
it's not me. It's fake.

The sound of a mighty rushing wind blowing. Moving in the holy ghost Anointing Power covered by the blood of Jesus.

Teach your daughter how to
be independent women who
can provide for themselves.

No weapon that is formed against thee shall prosper;
and every tongue that shall rise against thee in judgment
thou shalt condemn. This is the heritage of the servants
of the LORD, and their righteousness is of me, saith
the LORD." Isaiah 54:17 KJV

Thank you Jesus, yes, God, thank you Jesus.

Walk Better. Run Faster, Step- By- Step Always
Keeping God First Daily.

Kindness, compassion, love and respect for others, pass
it forward, In Jesus name.

Thank you Father for this news day, give us our daily blessing and daily bread cover and keep us safe.

With good will doing service, as to the Lord, and not to men:" Ephesians 6:7 KJV

Amen yes, God thank you for your teaching and the wisdom, knowledge understanding you entrusted me with and showing me how to use it wisely Amen thank you Jesus. Yes Lord, have your way in my life. Ebd

Father God, continue to send your Anointed Blessin to all those on this page, and the hands of those, who help along the way to help make this page possible. to continue to share your Anointed Grace, Mercy, Blessing, protection, healing, wisdom, knowledge and understanding. In Jesus Name I have Prayed.

2 Chronicles 13:5

"Ought ye not to know that the LORD God of Israel gave the kingdom over Israel to David for ever, even to him and to his sons by a covenant of salt?"

King James Version (KJV)

< > ▲ View Chapter

2 Chronicles 13:5 Context

2He reigned three years in Jerusalem. His mother's name also was Michaiah the daughter of Uriel of Gibeah. And there was war between Abijah and Jeroboam. 3And Abijah set the battle in array with an army of valiant men of war, even four hundred thousand chosen men: Jeroboam also set the battle in array against him with eight hundred thousand chosen men, being mighty men of valour. 4And Abijah stood up upon mount Zemaraim, which is in mount Ephraim, and said, Hear me, thou Jeroboam, and all Israel; 5Ought ye not to know that the LORD God of Israel gave the kingdom over Israel to David forever, even to him and to his sons by a covenant of salt? 6Yet Jeroboam the son of Nebat, the servant of Solomon the son of David, is risen up, and hath rebelled against his lord. 7 And there are gathered unto him vain men, the children of Belial, and have strengthened themselves against Rehoboam the son of Solomon, when Rehoboam was young and tenderhearted, and could not withstand them. 8And now ye think to withstand the kingdom of the LORD in the hand of the sons of

David; and ye be a great multitude, and there are with you golden calves, which Jeroboam made you for gods.

Amen thank you Jesus, I am grateful to you daily ebd

.

Corinthians 3: 13

"Every man's work shall be made manifest: for the day shall declare it, because it shall be revealed by fire; and the fire shall try every man's work of what sort it is."

King James Version (KJV)

< > ▲ View Chapter

1 Corinthians 3:13 Context

10According to the grace of God which is given unto me, as a wise masterbuilder, I have laid the foundation, and another buildeth thereon. But let every man take heed how he buildeth thereupon. 11For other foundation can no man lay than that is laid, which is Jesus Christ. 12Now if any man build upon this foundation gold, silver, precious stones, wood, hay, stubble; 13Every man's work shall be made manifest: for the day shall declare it, because it shall be revealed by fire; and the fire shall try every man's work of what sort it is. 14If any man's work abide which he hath built thereupon, he shall receive a reward. 15If any man's work shall be burned, he shall suffer loss: but he himself shall be saved; yet so as by fire. 1 6Know ye not that ye are the temple of God, and that the Spirit of God dwelleth in you Amen thank you Jesus. ebd

Yes, God I am thankful to you daily, all he right people for all the right purposes, and reason.

Everything is moving the power of God. Thank you Father, In Jesus name, yes Lord. Thank you. Amen.

John 1:5

"And the light shineth in darkness; and the darkness comprehended it not."

King James Version (KJV)

< > ▲ View Chapter

John 1 :5 Context

2The same was in the beginning with God. 3All things were made by him; and without him was not any thing made that was made. 4In him was life; and the life was the light of men. 5And the light shineth in darkness; and the darkness comprehended it not. 6There was a man sent from God, whose name was John. 7The same came for a witness, to bear witness of the Light, that all men through him might believe. 8He was not that Light, but was sent to bear witness of that Light.

2 Peter 3:14

"Wherefore, beloved, seeing that ye look for such things, be diligent that ye may be found of him in peace, without spot, and blameless."

King James Version (KJV)

< > ▲ View Chapter

2 Peter 3:14 Context

11 Seeing then that all these things shall be dissolved, what manner of persons ought ye to be in all holy conversation and godliness, 12Looking for and hasting unto the coming of the day of God, wherein the heavens being on fire shall be dissolved, and the elements shall melt with fervent heat? 13Nevertheless we, according to his promise, look for new heavens and a new earth, wherein dwelleth righteousness. 14Wherefore, beloved, seeing that ye look for such things, be diligent that ye may be found of him in peace, without spot, and blameless. 15And account that the longsuffering of our Lord is salvation; even as our beloved brother Paul also according to the wisdom given unto him hath written unto you; 16As also in all his epistles, speaking in them of these things; in which are some things hard to be understood, which they that are unlearned and unstable wrest, as they do also the other scriptures, unto their own destruction. 17Ye therefore, beloved, seeing ye

know these things before, beware lest ye also, being led away with the error of the wicked, fall from your own stedfastness.

Yes Lord Amen Amen Amen Thank you Jesus.

It's not about what you have, or may not have, it's about how you used what God have blessed you with wisdom wisely thank you Jesus.

Romans 8:28

"And we know that all things work together for good to them that love God, to them who are the called according to his purpose."

King James Version (KJV)

< > ▲ View Chapter

Romans 8:28 Context

25But if we hope for that we see not, then do we with patience wait for it. 26Likewise the Spirit also helpeth our infirmities: for we know not what we should pray for as we ought but the Spirit itself maketh intercession for us with groanings which cannot be uttered. 27And he that searcheth the hearts knoweth what is the mind of the Spirit, because he maketh intercession for the saints according to the will of God. 28And we know that all things work together for good to them that love God, to them who are the called according to his purpose. 29For whom he did foreknow, he also did predestinate to be conformed to the image of his Son, that he might be the firstborn among many brethren. 30Moreover whom he did predestinate, them he also called: and whom he called, them he also justified: and whom he justified, them he also glorified. 31What shall we then say to these things? If God be for us, who can be against us? Amen, Amen Amen Thank you Jesus.

Proverbs 18: 16

"A man's gift maketh room for him, and bringeth him before great men."

King James Version (KJV)

< > ▲ View Chapter

Proverbs 18:16 Context

13He that answereth a matter before he heareth it, it is folly and shame unto him. 14The spirit of a man will sustain his infirmity; but a wounded spirit who can bear? 15The heart of the prudent getteth knowledge; and the ear of the wise seeketh knowledge. 16A man's gift maketh room for him, and bringeth him before great men. 17He that is first in his own cause seemeth just; but his neighbour cometh and searcheth him. 18The lot causeth contentions to cease, and parteth between the mighty. 19A brother offended is harder to be won than a strong city: and their contentions are like the bars of a castle.

Amen Amen Amen thank you Jesus.

John 10:10

"The thief cometh not, but for to steal, and to kill, and to destroy: I am come that they might have life, and that they might have it more abundantly."

King James Version (KJV)

< > ▲ View Chapter

John 10:10 Context

7Then said Jesus unto them again, Verily, verily, I say unto you, I am the door of the sheep. 9All that ever came before me are thieves and robbers: but the sheep did not hear them. 9I am the door: by me if any man enter in, he shall be saved, and shall go in and out, and find pasture. 10The thief cometh not, but for to steal, and to kill, and to destroy: I am come that they might have life, and that they might have it more abundantly. 11I am the good shepherd: the good shepherd giveth his life for the sheep. 12But he that is an hireling, and not the shepherd, whose own the sheep are not, seeth the wolf coming, and leaveth the sheep, and fleeth: and the wolf catcheth them, and scattereth the sheep. 13The hireling fleeth, because he is an hireling, and careth not for the sheep.

Amen Thank you Jesus.

Psalms 16:1

"(Michtam of David.) Preserve me, 0 God: for in thee do I put my trust."

King James Version (KJV)

< > ▲ View Chapter

Psalms 16:1 Context

1 (Michtam of David.) Preserve me, 0 God: for in thee do I put my trust. 2O my soul, thou hast said unto the LORD, Thou art my Lord: my goodness extendeth not to thee; 3But to the saints that are in the earth, and to the excellent, in whom is all my delight. 4Their sorrows shall be multiplied that hasten after another god: their drink offerings of blood will I not offer, nor take up their names into my lips.

Yes God I am thankful to you daily Amen.

Proverbs 16:7
When a man's ways please the
LORD, he maketh even his
enemies to be at peace with
him.
King James Version (KJV)